WE JUST WANT TO BE LOVED!

A Message to My African-American Brothers

WE JUST WANT TO BE LOVED!

A Message to My African-American Brothers

By Delena Kay Flakes

We Just Want to be Loved!
By Delena Kay Flakes

Printed in the United States of America

ISBN# 978-0-6152-3933-0

Unless otherwise noted, all biblical references are taken from The New King James Version: Thomas Nelson Incorporated. © 1990; The New Open Bible, NKJV. Nashville: Thomas Nelson Publishers.

Cover photo courtesy of Jerry Wallace. He can be reached at publishing@ragenterprise.com

Cover model Chaundra D. Flakes

Other books by Delena Kay Flakes:

Worshippers Wanted! No Experience Necessary!

From the Head Down: Emotional Well Being for the Family

Aggressive Pursuit: Moving From Your Pit to Your Promise

Waiting for the Perfect Man (a Christian Romance Novel series)

For more information, go to: www.delenaflakes.com

R.A.G. Publishing and Production

Beaumont, Texas

www.ragenterprise.com

ACKNOWLEDGEMENTS

To God, my heavenly Father, thank You for allowing the gifts You have given me, to be used in this manner. Let these words speak to the spirit of the readers so as to cause them to love more and to expect more love. Let these words be inspirational and encouraging. I pray that a great change will come to those who read and receive what I have written.

To my husband, Garland; Thank you for loving me the way you do. I thank God for you. I love you. Your love for me inspires me.

To my mother, Ethel Ellis: You always encourage me to do the things I believe I can do, no matter what those things are. Thank you for your strength, for you have strengthened me.

Thank you, my sisters, my brother and my children: You all are my favorite cheerleaders!

Thanks to my friends for reading this book prior to its publication and thank you for encouraging me to publish it even though it contains strong topics.

Thanks to my dad, Ronnie Ellis, for your faith in me. Thank you for helping me to make my dream come true.

Thank you to Dr. Verlie Mitchell, Donna and Levi. I really appreciate all of your assistance to me on this project!

Thank you, Tracy Williams for all of your encouraging words and for helping me with this project. I have been inspired.

Thanks to all of you readers! Without you, all of this writing would be in vain. I pray that something in this book will speak to your hearts to encourage you, inspire you, or provide you with the insight to encourage someone else.

DEDICATION

This book is dedicated to all of my African-American sisters. It is especially dedicated to the ones who have worked hard to get where they are. I don't care if you are a manager at a local fast food restaurant or a chief executive for a major corporation. You can be a nurse or you can be the master surgeon. You can be a child care provider or a professor at a college. If you are more interested in earning a check as opposed to getting a check, this book is dedicated to you. If you have pushed and pressed your way to your present position and status, then I am dedicating this book to you!

This book is for the single African-American mothers, the grandmothers, the aunts and sisters who have reared their children by themselves, pushing them to be successful. This book is dedicated to the African-American mothers and wives who have sacrificed themselves for the benefit of her children and her husband.

This book is dedicated to the African-American mother who, in spite of the strikes against you, has persevered through the hard times. For the one who has learned how to stretch and make every dollar count, for the African-American woman who has pushed her children beyond her own achievements, to the one who has endured every hardship, this book is written on your behalf. I pray that I have heard your heart and your voice correctly. I hope that you will be blessed by the tears that I have shed in your honor, as I am putting these words on the pages of this book.

For the many nights you laid your head down after a long hard day of work—house keeping, cooking and quality time with your children—only to get a few hours' rest before you had to get up again and start another day, I commend you. For the many times you gave of your time, your love and your money, even when you couldn't afford to do so, I exhort you. For all of the times you've chastised your children and disciplined them so that they would be productive citizens, I praise you! For all of the work you've done, giving your son direction in order for him to become a strong African-American man, I thank you. For teaching your sons (and daughters) to say "please", "thank you", "yes, ma'am", "no, ma'am", "yes, sir" and "no, sir", may God's blessing for your obedience in training your children overtake you.

For all of the work you do, for purchasing this book and giving it to your son, my heart cries out in deep gratitude. I have four daughters who deserve to have a *good* African-American man.

FOREWORD

For as long as I can remember I have always been intrigued by purpose driven individuals. And, over the years my ability to recognize these persons has increased. I had not officially met Dr. Kay Flakes before I heard her say something that would profoundly affect me and the way I viewed my wife forever. She was able to do that in less than 3 sentences. So when we had a chance to meet later and I found out that she is the author of several books, I couldn't wait to read more of what she had to say.

This book; "*We Just Want to be Loved*", is a powerful and insightful commentary about the problems and/or dysfunctional ties in relationships between African-American men and women. To me, this book is a type report card to African-American men from the only ones other than God who could give one; the African-American woman. Who knows us and loves us more? Who supports us more? And, most of all, who is affected more? No one has more invested in us then our women. Kay, with this book, has given countless women a unified voice. A voice that says, "I know it hasn't been easy for you in this strange land, but I need you to be what God created you to be". This is a mighty WAKE UP CALL for brothers all across America. Before reading this book I thought, "This is for my sleeping brothers", but as I read it I realized I was awake only in some areas, and at best "sleepwalking" in the rest.

So Kay, I want to say thank you for showing us that black women still and always will love their black men. And that you love us too much leave us in the state we are in. We know even more now that our home isn't the penitentiary, but home is with our wives and children. It is not on the streets with our "homeboys"; but in church with our families. It is not creating gangs that tear down our neighborhoods; but creating businesses that build up our communities. Thanks for showing us how to go after our dreams instead of living out our nightmares. And for helping us to realize that movement doesn't necessarily mean progress. We have to plan our futures and strengthen our resolve. We must be involved in our children's lives. Understanding they need and desire our attention; our approval. Not many things we do in this life show our value or our contribution to this world more than the children that we raised.

But on a more personal note; before I read this book or should I say before I received my "report card", I thought I was doing pretty well. I was wrong. I see that by loving my God more, I can love myself better. Because of that I can love my queen and my children right. I am more determined to show even more self-control than selfishness. I will be more accountable. I will be more focused and yet more sensitive. I know and have known it won't always be easy but it's always worth it! Tina, Tracina and Stacy will always be worth it.

Finally, my African-American brothers, the charge has been given. I accept! DO YOU!!!!

Tracy Williams
Former Harlem Globe Trotter
President and CEO, Tracy A. Williams Enterprise, Inc.

WE JUST WANT TO BE LOVED!

A Message to My African-American Brothers

Chapter 1

MOMMA, WHAT'S WRONG WITH ME?

〜 ✑

"Momma, what's the matter with me?" my twenty-one year old daughter asked.

Putting down my spoon and lowering the fire on the stove, I took my attention from the pot of mustard greens I was cooking and gave my full attention to my daughter. I could tell by the tone of her voice that she really needed to talk to me about something.

"What's the matter, my baby?" I asked, as I pulled out a chair for her at the kitchen table and motioned for her to take a seat. After she slid into the chair, I took my seat close to her. I wanted her to know by my actions, that she had my complete and undivided attention.

"What is it about me? Why don't the guys like me?" she asked through an obvious tremble in her voice.

"There is absolutely nothing wrong with you," I honestly responded. "What has happened to you that would even make you ask that question?"

"There must be something wrong with me! Are my lips too big? Is it because I have dark brown eyes and not blue ones?" My daughter paused briefly before she continued. As she spoke, I listened attentively. I knew that her question was rhetorical and she really didn't want me to answer it. As she let out a heavy breath, I continued to give her my attention in silent anticipation and she continued to verbalize her frustrations.

"Maybe it's because my hair is short and curly instead of being straight and all down my back. Maybe it's because my hips are full and my breasts are larger than the other girls! Momma, I need you to explain to me why I can't even get a brother to look at me! And the ones who pay a little attention to me seem to take advantage of me and treat me like dirt! I am to the point where I think they just don't like the color of the skin I'm in!" She finished her last statement, put her face in her hands and let out a deep breath.

About that time, my sister entered the kitchen. "The reason you can't find a brother is because all of them are locked up in jail or out there mugging and thugging and are on their way to jail. Not only that, but nowadays, brothers are sleeping with brothers and they don't want you! Don't you know that the two most unmarried groups of people are African-American women and Asian men? So, honey, if you want a man you got to be willing to settle for one of them sweet and sour, egg roll eating fellas from China, or settle for an old white man, you know, get you one that's short and wrinkled with a little time left to live and a whole lotta money to leave you!" At the completion of Pearl's statements, she slapped her thigh, tossed her head back and let out a screech of a laugh. It was obvious by her words that she'd heard the conversation between Carmen and me. Pearl's comments didn't help. Carmen's muffled cries could be heard even though she tried to cover them with her hand.

"Hey, my baby," I said as I handed her a paper towel to dry her eyes. "Tell momma what happened so that I can maybe help you think through this thing."

Carmen dried her tears and shared her story. "Momma, you know me and Tyrone have been dating for a while, right?" I nodded my head and she continued. "Okay, two months ago was his birthday. I went to his house and told him I wanted to take him some place special. He let me blindfold him, but while I was driving him to the special place, he was fussing and complaining the whole time! I ignored his whining because I'd been planning his birthday surprise for a while and I wanted everything to be just right."

Tears started swelling up in Carmen's eyes. She grabbed another paper towel from the holder that was sitting on the table. She dried her eyes and continued.

"After I got to the port downtown, I grabbed my picnic basket out of the trunk of my car and led Tyrone up to the tower. Since Tyrone told me he's never been to the port, I thought it would be romantic to sit there, sipping our champagne, eating our cheese, fruit and crackers. I thought it would be nice to look over at the ship channel and watch the ships go by as the sun was going down. But, when we got to the top of the tower, and I took off the blindfold, he started fussing again and saying, 'Girl, why you got me up here? Where are we anyway? I thought you was taking me to my boy's house for a party or something! This is wack!' I couldn't believe how upset he was!"

"Even after I spread out the blanket and showed Tyrone all of the stuff I'd gotten for our picnic, his attitude never got any better. I mean, Ty had never been to the port and he'd never been on a picnic. I just wanted him to experience something different! All he could think about was his boys and partying with some white girls!"

Carmen took a deep breath and exhaled. I kept silent because I was sure there was more she wanted to say. During the brief break in Carmen's story, Pearl poured a glass of water for her. As she placed it in front of Carmen, she slid into the empty chair next to her. I hoped that she wouldn't try to add or interject any more of her rude comments about African-American men during the rest of Carmen's story.

"That's not the worst part," Carmen continued after taking a sip of the water. "The worst part was when I was taking Tyrone back home, he called his homies on his cell phone and told them how messed up his birthday was! Then, he made arrangements to meet up with them to play ball, even after I reminded him that I wanted to take him to a movie and spend more time with him! I mean, momma, what more am I supposed to do? I was even going to pay for the movie and everything!"

"When we got to his house, he just got out of the car, without kissing me goodbye or even thanking me for what I'd done. It took me a while but I finally got over it. But it all came flooding back to me when on today, my birthday, I called Tyrone to see what we were going to do, he told me he was on his way to Houston with his boys and they were going to be going to a club! When I reminded him that it was my birthday, he said, 'Oh, I forgot. I'll holla at'cha when I get back in a couple of days,' and he hung up without an apology or anything!"

"Why don't you just drop that bad monkey and get you somebody else?" Pearl snapped. As an African-American woman, she'd had her share of bad experiences, to include her most recent failed relationship where she found her man in bed with another woman.

"That's just the point, Aunt Pearl. There is nobody else available! It's like you said! So many brothers are already locked up! The ones who ain't locked up are on their way to jail because they are into gangs and they're thugs and dope dealers. The good ones who go to college end up with white chicks or Vietnamese girls. If the good guy does end up with a black girl, she's one of them light-brights with hazel eyes and sandy brown hair. You know, the ones that are so bright they could be white?" Carmen paused for a moment and took a visual survey of Pearl's and my expressions to ensure that we understood what she was talking about. We both nodded our heads and she continued her discourse.

"I mean, Aunt Pearl, momma, I'm a big girl with chocolate brown skin and short, naturally kinky hair! It's already hard for me to get a man to even look at me! I am always someone's last choice on the availability list. I'm just a regular kind of girl. There's nothing special about me. Not only that, but I love Tyrone and he says he loves me too. I just want him to really love me the way he says he does!"

The tears started rolling down Carmen's face again. Pearl reached over and gave her two paper towels. I got up from the table and started my tea kettle to warming. I knew our conversation was going to take more than just a few minutes. Carmen's story is a familiar one. She is not the first, nor do I think she will be the last, African-American woman who will feel unloved and rejected by her male counterparts. It is time for our African-American men to know how we feel.

Chapter 2

A MESSAGE TO OUR AFRICAN AMERICAN BROTHERS

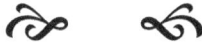

I am a writer. And, I am also a minister (servant) of the Gospel. For many years, I have heard the cries of women regarding their children, their husbands and many other matters affecting families and relationships. Several years ago, I started writing Christian Romance novels as a way to minister to young men and women about relationships. Being African-American myself, my novels tend to cater to the African-American audience, but the issues that the stories cover are common to people of all races, ages and cultures. The same holds true for this book. Although it is specifically directed toward African-American men, the contents and message of this project will still reach beyond racial barriers.

If I was going to write a Christian Romance novel about the subject matter that will be covered in this book, you would find the previously mentioned scenario within the pages of the novel. This book, however, is not a work of fiction. This book is a message to all of my African-American brothers and it comes directly from the heart of an African-American sister. I have ministered to many women over the years. Most of the women I have had conversations with, regarding relationships and family, have been African-American. This book is about some of our frustrations, our dreams, our desires and our prayers for you. It is a book about our love for you.

This book is written as a message to all of my African-American brothers, regardless of your age and financial status. You could be a preacher in the pulpit or you could be a bum on the streets. You could be a doctor or a lawyer. You could be in college or in jail. You could be my son, my father, my brother or my husband. You could be a man in high position or a janitor at a school. Whoever you are and wherever you are, it is my goal to reach out and touch every last one of you, my proud, powerful, strong and mighty African-American brothers. I pray that there will be something within these few pages that will inspire you and perhaps change your life.

For the most part, due to my extensive experience with incarcerated offenders, my message is for the many African-American brothers who are incarcerated, have been incarcerated or are on their way to being incarcerated because of their willingness to indulge in criminal activity. Additionally, I am writing to any African-American man who has room in his life to improve and grow. Let me begin this message to you all by saying, you are a rare breed, my African-American brothers! As such, you are very invaluable. There is none on earth like you. You are envied, admired and often imitated. You are versatile, creative, intelligent and multitalented.

You are unique. You are strong. You are influential and you are inspirational.

With everything you have going for you, we are frustrated beyond definition because of your willingness to live so far below your full potential. You have been created to be a king, yet you choose to be a pauper. Not only are you living as a pauper in the financial sense, but also in the educational sense. You have traded your years of learning for a life time of illiteracy and intellectual incompetence. You have traded your ability for compelling conversations for a vocabulary filled with slang and vulgarity. In the family area you have exchanged a life time of commitment for moments of perverted pleasures for the purpose of fulfilling your own selfish desires. You have exchanged your emotional stability for mental trips beyond your responsibilities through the use of illicit drugs and alcohol. Your political power has been greatly reduced by your never-ending cycle with felonious incarcerations and a lifelong commitment to parole and probation violations.

The point of this message is simple. It is a message to all of you, my brothers, from your African-American mothers, sisters, grandmothers, aunts, girlfriends, fiancées and wives. We have loved you from the day you were born and you have been missing in action for much too long. Don't you all realize you are the head of our homes? We want you to come home and take your place as Kings and Princes within our culture, within our communities and within our families. Our sons need you, our daughters need you, and we just want to be loved by you!

Chapter 3

BEGINNING AT AN EARLY AGE

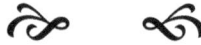

❧   ❦

I have been asked on many occasions, at what age should boys learn that they are boys and girls learn that they are girls. My response to this question has been that the learning and the training process begins at an early age. I am sure that any physician would tell you that a baby begins learning the moment she is born. As babies grow and mature, they learn. Whether we want to admit it or not, our children learn by watching, listening and imitating us. Our girls learn about womanhood and our boys learn about manhood through osmosis, soaking in everything they see, hear, smell, touch, taste and experience. We have learned about our different roles as males and females by watching others as they function in stereotypical as well as non-stereotypical roles. We see pictures which show us how to dress, and we are constantly bombarded with media presentations that show and teach us how to live. Children learn what they see and hear. Therefore, we as adults, have to be very careful about what we expose our children to.

One afternoon, I was in the kitchen cooking. My six year old god son was visiting. One of his favorite things to do is play video games. While I was cooking, he was in the den, which is next to the kitchen, playing his games and my four year old daughter was watching him.

While she was watching him exhibit his expertise on the controls, she engaged in encouraging conversation to let him know that he had her attention and support. Her conversation went something like this: "That's good, Little Jay. You are doing a good job on that game." And every time he would score a point, she would yell in her four year old voice, "You did it! You did it, Little Jay!" and she would jump up and clap her hands.

Little Jay would receive her compliments and encouraging words by responding, "Thank you," and he would quickly return his attention to his game. It was clear that he really appreciated her support. Whenever she would encourage him, Little Jay would make gestures, and grunt as if he was emphasizing the effort he was using in order to perform the way he did on the game.

After Little Jay reached a stopping point in his game play, Pumpkin invited him to play with her in her kitchen. Remember, I was cooking at the time. Little Jay accepted her invitation and followed her to the area where Pumpkin's kitchen was set up. Her kitchen was purposely set up near the real kitchen so that the two of us could cook at the same time.

As Pumpkin passed by me in the real kitchen, she came over to me and whispered, "Little Jay is going to play with me in my kitchen!" She had this great look of excitement on her face. The look reminded me of the way I felt the first time I cooked a meal for my husband.

Pumpkin immediately offered Little Jay a seat at her table and explained to him that she was going to cook something for him to eat. While he was waiting, Pumpkin offered Little Jay a coloring book and markers to entertain himself while she was preparing his meal. I laughed as I recalled that my husband would sometimes sit at the kitchen table and read over the mail or newspaper while I was in the kitchen preparing supper.

Little Jay busied himself with the coloring book and made small talk with Pumpkin as she pulled out plastic foods and dishes to make her playtime meal complete. During this process, Little Jay did the gentlemanly thing by complimenting Pumpkin on the clothes she was wearing and how nice her hair looked. He even made occasional comments regarding her meal, saying how "good" it "smells". It didn't take long for Pumpkin to complete her supper, prepare a plate for Little Jay and she placed the plate on the table in front of him. Little Jay put aside his coloring and "ate" his meal.

The entire scene made me realize, even more, how important parental guidance is when it comes to rearing our children. The problem that we have, as far as African-Americans are concerned, is that too many times, either the mother or the father is missing from the home, or both parents are missing and the children either learn from each other or they learn from bad examples. They learn from the television that they watch all day, they learn from the violent video games they play all day, they learn from rap videos, and they learn by watching the other thugs, hustlers and muggers on the streets.

This is not to say that *all* of our children are born to single parents and that all of our children are in this predicament, but it is to say that on too many occasions, they are! It also insinuates that our children are being reared by too many grandparents and substitute parents. Our children are being reared by older siblings because parents leave the home before the children wake up in the morning and the parents return home long after the children have gone to bed in the evening.

A friend of mine, who is an elementary school teacher, shared this story with me. On one occasion, she had a set of twins in her class. One of the twins was intellectually challenged as a result of her mother's substance abuse while she was pregnant with them. On many school mornings, the twins would wake up on their own. Their mother would sometimes be in the home, but she would be too intoxicated to perform her responsibilities as a mother. The smarter twin would dress herself and get her sister dressed. Then they would both walk to school.

The problem with this, in addition to the obvious, was the fact that the twins didn't know how to tell time. They would get up and get dressed whenever they were awakened. They would end up at the school at five in the morning and there would be no one at the school to let them in. Many times, they would come to the school late. Occasionally, the twins would show up at school on the weekends and holidays when the school was closed. When my friend tried to address the issues of tardiness with the mother, the results were negative. The sad thing about the whole matter was that both of the girls really wanted to be in school. They needed to be in school because it was the only place where they were sure to get a meal during the day.

My friend shared many stories like this one with me. One that haunts me the more I think about it is regarding "Reggie". Reggie was a student of my friend's who was constantly having family problems when he was in her elementary class. Although she tried to address the issues with the mother and later on with Child Protective Services, there was no relief for him. Reggie ended up in juvenile detention when he was about sixteen years old because he robbed a store at gun point. However, because of his age, he was released on probation. Due to the serious nature of the offense, his probation was an adult probation. After he was sentenced, he was released from the detention center and was told to go home. Of course, neither his mother nor father was present for his hearing nor was anyone there to pick him up when everything was said and done.

As a result of his abandonment, Reggie started walking home. The walk was a long one, so he "picked up" a bicycle on the way and rode the bike to his house. When he arrived home, he was not surprised to find the doors locked. He entered through an open window. Once inside, he was not surprised to discover that the electricity had been disconnected because the lack of utilities was something he had to deal with on a regular basis. The last straw for him was when he went to the refrigerator to get something to eat and he couldn't find anything.

Not having any money, he did the only thing he knew how to do. He went to a store and tried to steal something to eat. Of course he was apprehended and returned to the juvenile center. His probation was immediately revoked due to the commission of the new offense and he was sentenced to forty years in an adult prison. Many people would ask the question, "Where was his mother?" There is also another question that we have to ask, "Where was his father?"

To the African-American brothers, this scenario, although fictionalized to a small degree, is one that occurs on a regular basis. The African-American women who love you, give their bodies to you, bear your children, hope that you will be there to help them rear your sons and your daughters are, unfortunately, abandoned by you. When the mothers are abandoned, so are the many children you leave behind. And, on top of that, there are a great number of African-American children who have been abandoned by both of their parents as well!

Another thing that bothers me is the fact that you can father so many children and not acknowledge their existence. Or, maybe you do acknowledge them, but you don't see any problem with the fact that you have no real commitment to your children. You don't realize how painful it is for your child to not be able to identify who you are. Maybe the child knows you and knows your name, but the fact that you are his or her father is only supported by a few pieces of documentation. You have no real connection to your child. Now is the time for you to return to take your place in the lives of the children you have fathered! If you have what it takes to father them, you should take the time to love, protect, train, and teach them.

Let me share something with you. My children are often asked about their family status. Apparently, other children, and sometimes adults, find it hard to believe that all of them have the same last name. Children and adults alike have asked them the questions, "All ya'll got the same momma? All ya'll got the same daddy, too?" It is a sad day when children being born to married parents have become the exception rather than the norm.

In today's time, it is becoming more of the norm where children call others their siblings, knowing that they share only one parent. But, can you imagine how confusing the conversation regarding siblings would get when more than three parents are involved? Can you imagine how a child would feel when his siblings were picked up by their father for a weekend of fun, but he had to stay home because the man who picked up his brother and sister was not his father? Children would have half-siblings and non-siblings in a family. Children would grow up not knowing all of their siblings. Children would grow up feeling incomplete. Their family structure ends up being one big ball of confusion.

Think about it for a minute. Michael would bring his friend, David, home after school and he would introduce David to his brother, Simon. After saying their "Hello's," David would look over and see a picture with Michael, Simon and another boy hanging on the wall.

"Who's this boy in the picture with ya'll?" he'd ask out of honest curiosity.

"That's my brother," Michael would explain.

"So," David would conclude, "you and Simon have another brother!"

Simon would quickly explain, "No, that's Chance. Chance is Michael's brother, but he ain't my brother."

With that explanation, a look of confusion would grow across David's face. "What do you mean that Chance ain't your brother? If you and Michael are brothers, then you and Chance ought to be brothers!"

"Well," Michael would begin to explain, "me and Simon got the same momma, that's why he's my brother. But, we got different daddies. Chance and me got the same daddy, but we got different mommas. So, that's why Chance and me is brothers but Chance and Simon ain't."

David is confused, but he accepts the explanation given by Michael. But, before he has satisfied his curiosity, he sees another picture with Chance, Michael and three girls. "So, who are these girls in this picture? Why isn't Simon in the picture with ya'll?"

"AARRGHH!" Michael would groan in frustration as he walks over to the picture hanging on the wall. "This one right here," Michael explained as he pointed, "is me and Chance's sister 'cause we got the same daddy. This one is Chance's real sister 'cause she got our daddy, but Chance and her got the same momma, too. This one is Chance's sister, but not my sister 'cause they got the same momma but a different daddy. Simon ain't in the picture 'cause Chance's momma took us to get the picture and she didn't take Simon, cause she don't know Simon and she took me 'cause Chance told her I was his brother! Now, c'mon and let's go play some basketball!" Michael would let out another big heave as he tries desperately to change the conversation. He knows from experience that the next turn of the conversation would be questions regarding the whereabouts of Michael's father. Michael didn't want to have to explain that his father is in prison for having sex with a sixteen year old girl who is about to give birth to yet another one of his siblings. This scenario is so confusing to me that I can hardly keep it straight on the paper! Can you imagine how frustrating it would be to a child?

My husband and I accepted custody of our youngest daughter when she was only two years old. She started calling my husband "daddy" from the moment we brought her into our home. I don't think she ever knew her father, and I am sure that she started calling my husband "daddy" after hearing my children and following suit. The thing that hits me as strange is the fact that she didn't call me "mommy", as my children did. She called me her "auntie".

Shortly after we started taking her to day care, she started asking where her mother was. I understood the reason behind her question when I picked her up one evening. I heard another child ask her about her mother. Pumpkin would not answer the question. Later that evening, she asked me if I would be her mother. I told her that I would be her mother if she wanted me to be. Although having a mother was important to Pumpkin, I had to grow on her. However, having a daddy was more important to her as she instantly bonded with my husband.

I know that you may be thinking that I am being hard on the African-American men and that I am placing too much of the responsibility on you. But, in the past, all of the blame and responsibility have been placed on the African-American women. We need you to be responsible. We need you to be everything you promised you would be when you were taking our bodies for your own pleasure.

Chapter 4

THE BLAME GAME

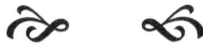

ã€€ã€€

*P*eople have been blaming other people for their failures, their faults, their actions or their lack of action since Adam blamed Eve in the Garden of Eden! My African-American brothers, you also blame others for the mistakes you have made. Mistakes become problems when we don't take responsibility for our own actions. In the same fashion that Adam blamed Eve and Eve blamed the serpent, we pass the buck, so to speak, when we are confronted with our deeds. We all make mistakes so I'm not addressing your imperfection. What I am addressing is the fact that you hesitate, if not avoid altogether, to take responsibility for your actions and behavior.

In the blame game, like Adam and Eve, we tend to blame those who are closest to us. Students blame teachers, saying, "That teacher just doesn't like me," whenever they perform poorly in school. Employees blame supervisors, saying, "My boss has had it in for me for a long time," when they are fired or faced with disciplinary action for their lack of performance on the job. Husbands blame wives, wives blame husbands and the children, and the children blame the parents. Criminal offenders blame "the system" and they blame society. Rich people blame the poor people, poor people blame illegal aliens and minorities, minorities blame all of the aforementioned. Passing the blame may result in a temporary self reprieve, but sooner or later, we will be faced with the consequences of our own action. If you remember, in the book of Genesis, in the end, God held Adam, Eve and the serpent each responsible for their own actions. And, each of them had to suffer their own consequences (Genesis, chapters 1-3). Adam was forced to till the soil, Eve's child birth was increased in severity, and the serpent was forced to crawl around on his belly and eventually he was going to be destroyed for his deception.

With your self-annihilation, self-destruction and self-suicide, no one has to worry about being fearful of your power! All other races of men are looking at you and watching. You give up on being strong and successful without even trying! You defeat yourself with your negative self-evaluation. When seeking after the things you have to work hard for, you get tired before you get started and you give up. When your dreams turn into nightmares, you blame everyone and everything around you.

You blame the white man for your lack of skills and education. If the truth is to be told, you all are dropping out of school like fleas dropping off of a dipped dog! It is as if you can't wait to leave the public educational system that your forefathers fought hard for so that you would have the same educational opportunities as your other racial counterparts. You blame the "system" and the teachers for your failures, but the truth is that no one is holding a gun to your head, forcing you to leave the school. No one *forces* you <u>not</u> to read a book or <u>not</u> to do your homework! Therefore, you are responsible for your own success or failure.

Fellas, ask yourselves the question, "How many times did my mother tell me to do my homework and I shrugged it off". How many times did your teacher assign you homework and you disregarded the instructions, went outside and played basketball instead? How many times did you bring home D's and F's on your report card and your mother punished you, but you still didn't do any better the next time? Have you ever asked for help? Did you ever indicate that you were having problems? Yet and still, when you have failed to reach your academic potential, you make yourself out to be the victim of a victimless and crimeless situation. There are no crimes being committed and there are no victims when it comes to high school drop-out rates among African-American men. There are only laziness, slothfulness and rebellion.

I know that many times, you feel as if no one cares and you have no support. If that's the way you are feeling, look inside yourself and realize you have the potential to succeed and you can become your own cheerleader! In your life, there will be times when you will bend over backwards to get a job done. You will stay the long hours, put in the extra effort, do your job and someone else's, and when all is said and done, either no one will be there to recognize your sacrifice, or someone else will take credit for what you have done. Don't dismay. You can still pat yourself on the back. Be satisfied in knowing that if no one else knows the work you've done, you will know. If you don't feel good about the work that you do, perhaps you should either reevaluate your work ethics and standards or reevaluate the work that you are doing.

As far as doing well in school is concerned, I am almost sure that if you would show some care and concern for your education, there would be a teacher, counselor, principal, or fellow classmate who would show you the same care and concern.

No matter what, just remember it's never too late for you to learn! If you don't have your high school diploma, you can still get your GED, if you are willing to do the work. There are many offenders who have come to the Texas prison system with little more than a fifth grade education. But, there are also many who have obtained their GED's and some have even taken college courses while they were incarcerated. No, I don't want you to come to prison so that you can obtain your education! I just want you to realize that if an offender can do it, so can you! With the right attitude and desire to succeed, you can overcome and defeat the blame game and its influence over your educational success.

I already know that you are intelligent, so I know that the problem does not lie in your lack of intelligence. Some of you are scientist and chemical engineers. You know how to take a powder substance, mix it, cook it and cut it so that it will turn into a rock formation that increases its value. You know how to mix simple over the counter drugs and household chemical agents with ether or some other substance in order to produce a product so powerful that it greatly interferes with your brain's ability to think. The planning and ingenuity that it takes for you to put together your greatest criminal heist are greater than the intellectual ability of many professional planners and strategists.

You have the intellectual ability to memorize large playbooks that have been authored by your football coach. You have the ability to learn and recite long renditions of poetry that has been set to the beat of a drum.

You practice the sport of basketball so that you are able to play with skill that many only hope and dream about. You have the intellectual ability to memorize the many secret passages, locks and clues that help you to win the many video games you play. You have the intellect to dream dreams and realize that there is more to life than where you are right now.

Additionally, I don't believe that the problem lies within your lack of ability or your lack of faith in yourself. I believe the problem lies within your inability to have faith in yourself to reach a positive goal. Let me share this with you. If you can envision yourself doing something, then you know that it is something that you really want, a dream that you can make a reality. If you can see it in your mind, you can believe it in your heart. If you can believe it in your heart, you can achieve it! Don't take my word for it! Close your eyes. Do you see yourself sitting in a classroom? Are you paying attention? See yourself understanding every word that is coming out of the teacher's mouth! Go further than that and see yourself studying and passing your test. See your grade. Don't stop there! See yourself as you walk across the stage, wearing your cap and gown, as you receive your diploma (or your degree if you want to pursue college)!

As I stated earlier, I am a writer. Whenever I sit down to write a book, I don't imagine just the first page. I don't imagine just the first *words* on the page. When I first sit down to my computer, I imagine the whole book! I see the cover, I see the chapters formatted, I see the title and I see the completed work which includes my picture on the back! I have an idea in my mind about how the completed project will look.

As I write my book and it begins to take shape, my dreams and my visions regarding the final product increase. I see myself opening the boxes that contain my work. I see the places where I will hold book signings. I see myself signing autographs. I envision book interviews, book reviews and press releases. All of these visions encourage my faith. I see myself doing it and I pursue my dream!

Think about this principle for a minute. Before you eat something, before you smoke a cigarette, drink a beer, view pornography, smoke crack, or engage in same sex sexual activity, you see yourself engaging in that behavior. You think about it and you dream about it. The more you engage in your mental motivational presentation, the more you want to pursue that thing you are dreaming about. The more you visualize yourself doing it, the more you *want* it and the more you are driven to *get* it or do it. As a matter of fact, you will not be satisfied until you reach your goal!

With all of the offenders that I have had the opportunity to interview or talk with, the one who exemplifies this method of progress the most is the one who is addicted to crack cocaine. From many conversations, I have learned that a crack addict wakes up in the morning and the only thing on his mind is getting his next fix. The crack addict envisions himself obtaining his drug of choice despite any obstacle that he may be faced with. If he doesn't have any money, he will create ways to make money. Don't be fooled. The crack addict will loan out his car to the drug dealer and allow the drug dealer to beat him up so that he can tell his wife or his mother that his car was stolen, just to get his fix. He will wash windshields, cut grass, take out your trash, change the oil in your car, walk your dog, and even sell his body for sexual favors, just to get enough money to get a hit. The crack addict will even steal something for you; all you have to do is tell him what you want and the size you want it in. His goal and all of his daily activities are centered around his desire to reach his destination and he will not let anyone or anything keep him from it. After he has obtained his money, he will walk miles to find the dealer so that he can spend the money he desperately earned, so that he can smoke it away in as little as five minutes.

It is easy to see how this aggressive method of accomplishment can work for negative behavior. What do you have to lose by applying this same method to some of the positive things in your life that you have only thought about? Dare to dream beyond your circumstances and dare to dream beyond your limited imagination!

Back to the blame game. Not only do you blame the white man, but you blame the Hispanics for taking away your jobs and employment opportunities. One thing I have observed about Hispanics is, although they commit their share of criminal offenses, they will work at whatever job they have to in order to get what they need. They are willing to work at the dirty entry level positions. Look around your neighborhood. Where do you see them working? I've seen them standing in groups on the street corners, early in the morning, waiting for someone to pick them up for a construction or field job. They will pick cabbages, watermelons, lettuce and cantaloupes. And they would even pick cotton if it wasn't for the cotton gin machine. I've seen them working in the heat of the day, on our highways and city streets. They pick up trash, lay asphalt, and cut grass. I've seen Hispanics washing dishes at restaurants. They have served me at fast food restaurants and they have cleaned up behind me at hotels and motels. They have served me in a plethora of locations and they have asked for little in return for their services. They show up on time, work all day, and they will catch a ride, catch the bus, walk or ride a bicycle in order to make it to their job location.

Many of you have told me that you don't want to start at the beginning. I've heard you say that you weren't "diggin' no ditches," and you "ain't flippin' no burger neither!" I want you to realize that you have to start somewhere. The only way you can finish anything is to start. But, also remember that the way you start or where you start does not mean you will end there. You could start out on the yard squad today and end up as the landscape supervisor in a few years.

If there are a lot of illegal aliens working in your neighborhood, and if you feel that someone in your area is hiring more Hispanics than brothers, challenge the business owner and ask for a job! The business owner may be looking for willing applicants to fill jobs quickly. If you show that you have a true desire to work hard, someone will be willing to hire you. No matter what the pay may be, there is no shame in earning an honest dollar. Even I started out working at a fast food restaurant.

You blame the whites, you blame the Hispanics and you blame the Asians for robbing you of any entrepreneurial spirit you may have had. Let's face it! Many of you have the drive to be a successful small business owner. You even have the drive to be the owner of a large corporation or enterprise. You have started your own street pharmaceutical business, you've started your own apparel retail business, you've sold appliances that you have stolen, and you've sold cars and car parts from vehicles you have carjacked and stripped. You know how to illegally mass produce videos and musical CD's. You have set up on empty lots, and you have even gone door to door, passed out flyers, and hung up posters in order to sell your product. You know what you need in order to run a successful business.

You have worked well into the night to package your products to make them more appealing to potential customers. You know how to advertise and you know how to solicit customers. You even know how to meet the supply and demand for your product and you know how to watch the market and price your merchandise accordingly. You also know how to take your profits and reinvest them back into your business.

The problem with your entrepreneurial spirit is not that it has been taken away. It has only been misused and misplaced. The biggest problems that law enforcement has with your businesses is: #1 –the product you sell (i.e. drugs, stolen merchandise, boot legged videos, etc.), and #2–the fact that you have not set up a proper business structure (i.e., a DBA, tax ID number, employee ID number, etc.).

In my profession, I have witnessed and interviewed some of the greatest entrepreneurs. One offender I talked with was "dealing purses". He was legally obtaining his merchandise from a wholesaler in one state and he was selling his products in Texas. The problem with his merchandise was the fact that he was selling his "knockoffs" as the real thing! In other words, he was committing fraud! As the investigation into his business continued, law enforcement also discovered that the offender did not have his business registered, he was selling without the proper documentation, and he was not reporting his taxes! The problem was not the business itself, but it was the way he was handling his business.

If you want assistance in order to legitimize your business, you can go to the internet and conduct a search by entering the words "small business assistance", or "small business association". You can also go to your local library and ask for assistance in finding books that can teach you how to start your business. Some colleges have small business assistance centers on their campuses. Many times, this assistance is free. You work hard at building an illegal empire. You can achieve the same, if not greater, financial success if you would channel that energy into something legal.

Think about it for a minute. The Asians already know the power of your dollars! This is why they set up businesses in your neighborhoods! They open businesses that offer services to you such as nail shops. They open up businesses that sell our African-American hair care products. They even sell clothing and shoes that are to our liking. They open up restaurants and when you don't eat their oriental dishes, they offer fried chicken and barbecue ribs on their menu to cater to your pallet! I have been told, that the Asians set up their businesses in the African-American neighborhoods purposely, knowing that you will spend your money on food, clothing and hair care products. They want you to only pay in cash and will not accept your checks or credit cards. They set up businesses in your neighborhoods, knowing that you will patronize them before you patronize each other. When will you advance beyond your crablike mentalities and open up legitimate businesses that will satisfy the needs of your own people?

One of the first steps you can take in order to build your business is get a notebook or spiral tablet. Begin writing down everything you can think of regarding the type of business you want to own. Write down several names for your business. Identity your customer base—who do you want to sell your services or products to. Identify where you want to open your business. Check out your competition. Ask yourself the questions; "What can I do better?" or "How is my business going to be different or set apart from the competition in my area?" Set up goals for your business. What do you want to accomplish by the end of your first, second, fifth, and tenth years in business?

Every time you think about your business, write it down. This process will help you identify your passion. If you have a passion for your business, you will be excited about it. You will have pages of information about your business. You will be able to measure your level of dedication for your business by the amount of information you have inside of you that ends up in your notebook. You will also know how plausible your business is. Additionally, you will be adding substance to your dreams. This substance will help you to make your dreams come true! Furthermore, when the time comes, you will have the makings of, or the elements of, a business plan.

Take the time to legitimize your business. Go to your chamber of commerce and obtain information regarding starting your small business. Go to your county courthouse and register your DBA (Doing Business As) name. You can find information and forms for obtaining a tax ID and employee ID number by searching the internet or going to a small business help center in your area. If you can't find it through any of these entities, email me and I will send the link to you! If you can't email me, write me and send a self addressed stamped envelope and I will send you the forms! My email address and mailing address are at the end of this book. Why would I do that? You are my African-American brothers. I love you! I don't want to tear you down; I want to build you up. I recognize your power and your potential. And, I am your keeper.

Secondly, design your business card. If you don't have computer skills, you can pay your niece or nephew a few dollars to do this for you. Print your cards out and begin passing them around. Tell everyone you know that you are going to be in business. Give them your projected start up date. When you do this, you will know how much support you are going to have by the way people respond to you, and you will be starting your customer base.

Whenever I begin a book project, I follow the methods that I am giving you. I start by writing down everything that comes to my mind about the book, first. Once I have written down everything that comes to my mind, I look back over my "notes" and see what I can add. By the time I finish my notes, I have an outline of the book from start to finish. At that point, I sit down at my computer and begin typing. The next thing I may do is design the cover of the book or select the title.

I don't start trying to sell my books after they have been printed, I start selling them as soon as I have the book outlined and the cover has been designed. I identify my potential readers and I share a few pages of the book with them. I determine if I am going to complete the book or change something about the book by the way they respond. After my brief presentation, I give my customers a potential release date. When I obligate myself, I am more pressured to complete my projects.

The next things you can do is drive around your neighborhood and identify potential buildings and locations for your business. You can go to your county courthouse and obtain a list of properties that are scheduled for demolition. Many times, these buildings can be purchased for a small amount of money and the building can be refurbished and brought up to code. When you do that, you will immediately have equity in your building and you can use that equity to obtain a loan against the property so that you will have funds to start your business. You already completed your business plan so you have what you need to go to a lender or look on the internet for possible grants.

I am not foolish. I know that by the time you finish reading this chapter, some of you will be motivated and you will get started on the dream that you have been keeping as a secret in your heart for a long time. However, many of you will consider the words on these pages are as much of a fantasy as your dreams are. As I stated earlier, no one has to take anything from you. You blame everyone and everything around you for your lack of achievement and your lack of success. But, the truth of the matter is, no one has to take anything from you because you are throwing away everything you have!

Chapter 5

GENOCIDE

☙ ❧

*F*ellas! What are you doing? Not only are you absent and we are calling for your presence, additionally, our message to you is to warn you about your genocidal tendencies! Don't you realize you are doing nothing but killing each other? You are already growing to be the smallest majority group in the United States, but instead of doing what you need to do to secure your future, you are destroying yourselves. Not only are you destroying yourselves, but you are causing the extinction of our people by your habits and self– destructive activities!

In addition to throwing away your personal success as mentioned in the previous chapter, you are also committing genocide! You may be asking yourself the question, "How are we committing genocide". Let me begin by putting it like this. African-Americans as a whole, make up only about 12.9% of the population in the United States, according to the year 2000 census (See *www.census.gov/prod/cen2000/doc*). In the state of Texas, according to the same census, African-Americans make up approximately 12% of the population. Yet, you make up approximately 30% of the offender population, according to the Texas Department of Criminal Justice Statistical Report Fiscal Year 2005 (published March 2006). According to the same report, African-American males make up approximately 30% of the newly received offenders into the Texas Department of Criminal Justice—Institutional Division, for the year 2005, which indicates that the incarceration rate for African-American men is not going down.

Many people are appalled when they read these types of statistics. Before I started working for the Texas prison system and before I accepted my position as a Sociologist, these statistics offended and angered me as well. I felt that all of our African-American brothers were being harassed and violated by the judicial system that was supposed to protect them. Over time, I have come to realize that if this was a time before and during the Civil Rights Movement, I believe I would have been justified in my feelings and opinion. But, as things are today, my position on the subject of the incarceration of African-American brothers has shifted. All of the blame for the numerous incarcerations of African-American brothers is not on the shoulders of others alone. We, too, are at fault and should be held accountable.

The reason for the change in my thinking is simple. As my years of experience with the prison system increased and as I have had more opportunities to interview and converse with offenders, white, Hispanic and black alike, I had to change my position. This is not to say that I have totally changed my position regarding the fairness, or should I say, the unfairness of our system of law and order, but it is to say that a good portion of the blame for our numerous and repetitious incarcerations is largely due to the number of crimes that African-American brothers commit. I am sorry for this revelation, but truth is a purging fire and once truth has been exposed, truth can be dealt with.

Based on many conversations with incarcerated offenders who did not have money to pay for an attorney, I am still of the opinion that African-American men are coerced into accepting plea bargained sentences, even when there are problems with the charges against them or when there were problems with their arrest. This is not to say that the offenders were innocent or falsely accused. It is to say that there have been occasions where there were due process problems with their arrest. This fast paced practice of plea bargaining and selling each other out (a.k.a. snitching), results in African-American men being incarcerated more expeditiously. I do agree that there is still racial discrepancy in sentencing practices and other aspects of our judicial system.

I still believe that African-Americans, especially the men, are singled out more often than people of other races due to the fact that I have been the victim of racial surveillances while shopping. I have also been the victim of "D.W.B.", (Driving While Black), on more than one occasion.

What caused this drastic shift in my thinking and opinion was not due to my personal experiences, or due to some statistical research that I uncovered. The thing that caused the greatest change in my opinion was the offenders themselves. As a Sociologist for the prison system, I had the opportunity for many one-on-one interviews with convicted felons. It was the confessions out of the mouths of our African-American brothers that caused me to realize that, for the most part, our brothers are causing their own demise, as they have unashamedly confessed and shown me that almost every last one of them is guilty of the offenses they were accused of committing! Even at that, many of my African-American brothers who were caught red handed still wanted to blame the "white man" for their arrest and incarceration. And, unknowingly, our African-American brothers are committing self-annihilation through self-inflicted incarceration!

I know you don't believe me so let me give you some examples. The stories I am about to share with you are not figments of my imagination, but they are generalities of our brothers' behavior in the criminal world! Firstly, African-American men end up in prison for many of the same crimes as men of other races. African-American men use and sell drugs, they burglarize homes and buildings, jack cars, rob convenience stores, they snatch ladies purses, shoplift (boldly, I might add), they beat up their girlfriends, they hit their mothers and other people, and steal cars in broad daylight. African-American brothers also drive while they are drunk, carry weapons illegally, and, I am ashamed to say, they rape women and children, and they kill people.

For the most part, these crimes are bad in and of themselves. Our African-American brothers increase the magnitude and impact of their offenses by adding a gun during the commission of the crime. In Texas, a crime committed while brandishing or simply being in possession of a gun or other weapon can have a great impact on the type and length of sentence that will be handed down.

Another reason our African-American brothers make up an alarming percentage of the inmate population is because of the foolishness in which they commit their offenses. According to many offender confessions, when our African-American brothers sell drugs, they do so, on the street corners, in public, during daylight hours! Additionally, everybody in the neighborhood knows you are selling drugs because you publicize your business! Not only is this a foolish practice, but whenever you see a police officer coming your way, you run! This gives a police officer immediate "reasonable suspicion" to chase you and arrest you. While you are running from the officer, you attempt to rid yourself of any evidence by tossing everything out of your pockets as you are running. This gives the officer further leverage against you because after you are chased down and placed into custody for Evading Arrest, the police officer will search the area and possibly find more drugs than you were initially in possession of. You will be charged with whatever he finds. And, if the officer finds nothing, you still have the charge for fleeing from him! In the state of Texas, Evading Arrest could equal up to 2 years in a state jail facility.

My brothers, you have even told me, during those many conversations, that you also use your drugs in public! You've been arrested outside of convenience stores for smoking crack under a "No Loitering" sign. You have been arrested at school for smoking marijuana. I have personally witnessed you smoking a blunt in the movie theater, in a restaurant, and even in the grocery store.

You use and sell your drugs in public and you foolishly think your boldness is courage. You foolishly and/or boldly enter a store in broad daylight, grab an armload of clothing and run out of the store, thinking that you shouldn't get caught. You rob gas stations in your own neighborhood where there are video cameras. Since it is your neighborhood, there are witnesses who know who you are and they will gladly turn you in for the few dollars they are offered by the Crime Stoppers organization.

Let's look at that one for a minute. What does it profit you to rob a convenience store at gunpoint? You always get less than one hundred dollars and you almost always get a lot of time for committing the crime! Here is a scenario that will open your eyes: You rob a store and get $500 (I'm being generous). You are captured and convicted. Your aggravated 7 years sentence is going to have to be served day for day, with no credit for good behavior. If you take $500 and divide it by 7 years (again I'm being generous), that's approximately $71.43 per year. Divide that by 12 months and you get about $5.93 per month! If you divide that amount into weeks and days, you see quickly that your criminal offense was worth less than a few cents per hour! You could make that much money in a few hours by simply raking leaves or cutting grass! And, you wouldn't have to go to prison after you did it!

You have burglarized homes that belong to your neighbors and then you boldly sell your neighbor's TV, VCR and microwave oven to their friends! You have even taken things from and stolen from your African-American mothers, sisters and grandmothers! The insanity of your dilemma is that you blame your fall on everything and everyone around you, without taking a look at your own influences towards your destructive behavior. This is insane and it has got to stop!

In addition to the blame games you play, you also make up all kinds of excuses for your behavior. I have heard all kinds of excuses and you are the master when it comes to creating them! You give more excuses than a bank has pennies! Let me tell you what your excuses are: Excuses are like cotton candy. They are full of fluff, sweet, easy to make, but when you get right down to it, it's empty and good for nothing!

One of your biggest criminal defenses is that you were doing what you "needed to do to survive"! News flash: selling drugs and getting high are not survival skills! Stealing my car is not a survival skill! Robbing a convenience store is not, has never been and never will be a survival skill! Joining a gang is everything but a means to survive. Sitting under a bridge, holding a sign that reads, "will work for food", is NOT a survival *skill!*

I've seen people doing what they needed to do in order to survive. There is a woman that I admire. She dresses colorfully with her skirt, blouse, sweater vest, and her hat. She generally has on a pair of rain boots to complete her outfit. On a regular basis, I see her outside of different business establishments, sweeping the pavement and parking lots, earning whatever she can in order to survive! Whenever I see her, she's always singing and she is always in a good mood. If you pass by her and honk your horn, she will always take the time to look up and wave at you! She is a woman to be admired. She is an African-American woman. She is a survivor!

To survive, I've seen a woman in a wheel chair, slowly going along the street, gathering aluminum cans. I've seen people going through trash cans and dumpsters gathering aluminum cans and other aluminum articles, in order to survive. I've watched men wash windows and hose down parking lots in order to survive. People walk miles to get to a job, in order to survive. Many of you, my African-American brothers would not do the things you feel are beneath you in order to survive. Guess what! If you are already on the bottom, there is nothing beneath you! The only way for you to go is up!

As college graduates, my husband and I have found ourselves in positions where we did what we needed to do in order to survive. We have gone without cable. We have moved from our large five bedroom, three bath home in the *good* part of town, to a small three bedroom, two bath shack on the "Westside" in order to survive. We have gone from driving and having in our possession three vehicles at a time to where we have had only one car that we all had to share. There was a time in our lives when we, two college graduates, cleaned toilets at a school at night, in order to survive and take care of our children! Don't tell me what you can't do! As my mother has taught me, can't is synonymous, many times, to *won't!*

Let me give you another example of survival. There is a man I know of, an African-American brother, who started out as a boy, cutting lawns with his grandfather. He saw how much money his grandfather was making and he saw how much money his grandfather was paying him. At that point, he started saving his money while his cousins spent their money on chips and ice cream. He saved until he had enough money to purchase his own lawnmower. He got to the point where he hired his cousins to work for him. His business grew to the point where he was repairing lawnmowers and that grew to repairing vehicles. Over the course of time, he started working at different jobs that related to cars sales industry. With proper money management, learning everything that he could, and properly investing in himself, he grew his business into a profitable empire. His business was so profitable, that years later, he was financially able to purchase a car dealership that is worth millions!

The most inspiring story that I can share with you, regarding survival, is about a man that my husband and I met recently. When we entered the Jefferson County Airport, we saw a man with a small frame, and salt-and-pepper hair, pushing the luggage cart. His bright yellow jacket was in need of pressing, but the man wore it with pride. On first appearances, the man looked to be about seventy-nine years old, or so. We took our seats as we were waiting for our flight to be called, and we watched the African-American man go back and forth, pushing the luggage cart. We both agreed that at his age, it was inspiring to see the man still in good health and working.

After watching the man for a while, my husband's curiosity got the best of him. He wanted to know for sure how old the man was and he wanted to engage the gentleman in some casual conversation about his life and work history. My husband introduced himself and learned that the man's name was Leon. He asked Leon a few general questions and made a few comments about the weather. Then, he bluntly asked Leon how old he was. Leon quickly and with a smile on his face, said, "Guess!"

My husband's guess was on his lips when another gentleman entered the airport. It was obvious that the other man had overheard at least part of the conversation between my husband and Leon, because he quickly responded to my husband's question. He said, "That's my friend! He's been my friend for over fifty years! He's one hundred and two years old!" The man made his comments, pointed and winked at Leon, and walked on towards the counter to check his bags. Needless to say, my husband stood there, with a shocked look on his face. I was left with my mouth hanging open.

At one hundred and two years of age, Leon was still working as the airport's porter. There was a newspaper article and a small recognition plaque hanging on the wall in the airport that provided us with more information about Leon. Leon told us that he'd been employed with the airport since about 1961. When he turned one hundred, Leon said he bought himself a truck. He bragged about the fact that, even at his age, he was still able drive himself wherever he wanted to go, he could still see without his glasses (he did need them in order to read, however), and, he proudly stated, "I don't owe nobody nothing!" Leon personifies the survival of the African-American man.

What you need to do is come up with some new survival skills. Getting a better education and/or completing your high school diploma or GED is a survival skill. Increasing your self-image will help to increase your self-worth and self-esteem. These are survival skills. Doing whatever you can do and need to do in order to get a job is a survival skill. I'm not talking about anything difficult. I'm talking about simple things like dropping the thug like attire, pulling up your pants and putting on a belt. Additionally, lose the grill! Contrary to popular belief, it's not cute! Neither is the nose ring, the tongue ring or any of those numerous tattoos you have! Some of you look so unprofessional when you show up for a job interview that it's scary! So scary in fact, that *you* wouldn't even hire you for a job!

Your willingness to work at whatever job you can get until you can get the job you want, is a survival skill. If you have earnestly tried and still can't get a job, create a job! Cutting lawns, cleaning yards, cutting down and removing trees, hauling trash are all jobs that you can do for other people and get paid!

Now, back to genocide through incarceration. Don't be fooled into thinking that you will be safe if you just don't hang around your fellow African-American brothers. I can share several stories with you that involve an African-American brother being in the company of a Caucasian male when "something went down." The truth of the matter is, if you are in an area where a crime is being committed, even if you had absolutely nothing to do with the offense, you stand a greater chance of being the only one arrested. Say, for example, you are in a car with your white friend and he gets pulled over for speeding. The officers suspect that there is cocaine in the car or some other drug. If the car is searched, even if the car and the drugs don't belong to you, you will be accused! If your white friend is the guilty party, it is his car, and his family is well known in the city, he has more to lose than you do. He will tell the officer in charge that the drugs were yours and you will go to prison because you don't have the money for a lawyer, and you believe that your white friend won't lie to the police! You will go to jail because, as far as your friend is concerned, you are expendable!

In order for you to decrease the numbers of African-American brothers in the penal systems across the United States, it is important that you all stop doing the things that will get you incarcerated! If you quit making it easy for police officers to accuse you and arrest you, they will have to do their hunting somewhere else. The reason we need you to stop your genocidal tendencies through self-imposed incarcerations is simple. If you are locked up and if you are kept away from us, who will take care of our daughters? Who is going to take care of and rear our sons? We, the mothers, grandmothers, sisters and aunts, can only teach our children (especially our sons) so much. The one thing that we can't do is teach our daughters how they should be treated by a man who says he loves her, and we can't teach our sons how to be that man. We need you to teach our sons to be strong African-American brothers!

Chapter 6

MESSAGE TO THE GANG-BANGERS

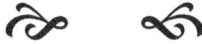

*B*loods. Crips. Gangster Disciples. Mandingo Warriors. Five-Deuce Hoova Crips. Six-Nine Crips. South Side, North Side, East Side and West Side. Red, Blue, Red-Black and Green. What does it all mean? What or whom does it benefit? How does it make you grow? How does it make you stronger? How does it make you prosper? And, somebody, please tell me how in the world does it get you respect? When you are in a gang, people don't respect you; they fear you and you intimidate them! Fear and intimidation do not make you a man. Fear and intimidation make you a thug who needs to be locked up! Being in a gang does not make you a man and it does nothing to help you succeed. The only thing that being a gang-banger offers you is death and destruction. This is just another method by which our African-American brothers commit genocide!

When I think about the original gangsters, I am reminded of people like Al Capone (www.crimelibrary.com, 2006). Even though he obtained great wealth, he cannot be considered successful. With all of his wealth and acts of intimidation and violence, he still ended up in prison and he died before his fiftieth birthday. This is the story of the gang-bangers. They end up in prison, they end up dead or both (i.e., they die in prison).

My African-American brothers, the more I learn about your gang activity, the more I realize that the only thing you all are succeeding in doing is killing each other. At least Al Capone clearly identified his enemies before he killed them. You all are engaging in drive by shootings in an attempt to kill someone you think has disrespected you and too many innocent bystanders become your victims. More often than not, the person who allegedly disrespected you was only calling you names that you call yourself. You call each other "dog", "fool" and "nigger", but as soon as someone else calls you by these words, your feelings get hurt.

Why do you have to call each other dogs and fools anyway? And, please tell me why do you call each other "nigger"? What does that word mean anyway? According to my son's Spanish I teacher, the Spanish word for black is "Negro" and has been long used to identify those of us with dark colored skin or those of us with African ancestors. I imagine that the word nigger came about when southern whites, who were low on the economic scale, pronounced the word "negra" instead of Negro. Then, I suppose, the word "negra" evolved, or should I say, degenerated into the word "nigger". This word, with all of it's negative connotations, has been used in conjunction with other negative adjectives to form compound words such as; lazy nigger, no good nigger, trifling nigger, slothful nigger, nigger rigging, ignorant nigger, sorry nigger, shucking and jiving nigger, just to name a few.

This word has never referred to anything good and I doubt that it ever will.

I put the word "nigger" in my web's browser. There were many web sites that came up as a result. Those web sites were related to web sites for "Black Jokes", "Nigger Jokes", the KKK, and other sites that promoted hostility towards blacks or African-Americans. The only web site that was helpful to me in my search for the historical use of the word and a possible definition was The African-American Registry® Copyright 2005, found at www.aaregistry.com. I obtained the following quote from this web site as I believe it states the sentiment of many African-Americans, male and female alike. "*Web searchers find what most Blacks know from personal experience, that nigger is an expression of anti-Black hostility. Without question nigger is the most commonly used racist slur during hate crimes*".

One thing is for sure. I don't want *anyone* to call me a "nigger", black, white, Hispanic, Asian, Arabian, it doesn't matter to me. I don't allow my children to refer to each other or their friends by that word. The word has always referred to African-Americans in a negative sense. I am more than a "nigger".

Bastard is a word that would cause you to defend yourself because of its negative connotation. But, when you think about it, the word "bastard", in common terms means a child born out of wedlock. For many of you, when a person identifies you as a bastard, that person would do so correctly. So, what you would be defending yourself against would be the negative connotation that the word implies. Just like you wouldn't want anyone to call you a bastard because of its negative connotation, you shouldn't want anyone to refer to you by any other negative, racially objective, racially hostile, epithet. My African-American brothers, when will you all stop referring to each other in this negative light? Others don't have to do it because we do it to ourselves.

In addition to killing each other over the loose and misunderstood use of the word "respect", you fight each other over high priced tennis shoes and basketball jerseys. You fight and kill because someone was selling drugs on your turf; an area, I might add, that does not belong to you. You are destroying yourselves and you can't see that. People of other races have been telling us for decades that we are killing each other as the number of black-on-black offenses are increasing. When are you going to stop and take note of what life experiences are telling us and stop this madness?

There was a time when I was asked to speak to a youth group. As I often do when I am speaking to young people, I asked them what they wanted to talk about. Of course they wanted to talk about sex and dating, but at this particular engagement, some expressed that they wanted to talk about the Bible's views on gangs. They indicated that there were several gang members at their school and they wanted to talk to their gang-member friends about Jesus. Whenever they tried to talk to their friends about their gang activity, the gang-banger would express that the Bible doesn't say anything about being in a gang. Fortunately, the Spirit of the Lord had provided me with Scriptural foundation on the subject of gangs, just a few days earlier. If you really want to know the end results to gang membership and gang activity, or you need scripture to substantiate the Bible's position on gang-related activity, all you have to do is turn in your Bible to Proverbs 1:10-19. These verses are as follows:

> **Proverbs 1:10 My son, if sinners entice you,**
>
> **Do not consent.**

This verse immediately identifies the audience of this perspective reading. It is addressing the same audience that I am addressing in this book, our African-American *sons*. It says, "If sinners entice you," don't consent. The scripture points out that *sinners*—plural—will try to entice you or recruit you. The plurality of the word sinner can easily translate to mean more than one person. More than one person can constitute a gang. Sinners can be easily identified as those who do things which contradict the Word of God. I believe we would all agree that killing, stealing, drug dealing, fighting, stabbing, raping and pillaging are all forms of *sin*. For the most part, gangs are built and organized on this particular philosophy. Gangs are geared towards robbing from the rich (and not so rich), and keeping it for themselves. This scripture provides the one reaction that our African-American brothers should consider when they are solicited by gang members to join up; "Do not consent!"

> **Proverbs 1:11 If they say, "Come with us,**
>
> **Let us lie in wait to shed blood;**
>
> **Let us lurk secretly for the innocent without cause;**

Verse eleven further describes the way gang members operate. Firstly, they need a group of people, as this verse says, "they say," which indicates there is always more than one person involved. This just let's me know that beneath their hard exterior, gang members are cowards! They rarely operate and commit their acts of violence alone!

The motive of the gang member is to "lie in wait to shed blood." A gang member will hardly face his enemy unless he has the protection of the rest of the cowards. Gang members are sneaky and will attack you when you least expect it. They don't operate in the gentlemen's fashion by challenging you to a duel. They will hide in dark alleys, catch you at your weakest point and then attack you like a savage beast. In the end, we discover that many of their attacks are unwarranted, unjustified, and they are always unbeneficial. This verse says that gang members sit and wait "for the innocent without cause." Many of the victims of gang violence are victims of random acts of violence. The victim's only offense was being in the wrong place at the wrong time. These ambush type tactics do not make men out of our African-American brothers. They only succeed in making gang members victims of their own stupidity.

> **Proverbs 1:12   Let us swallow them alive like Sheol, And whole, like those who go down to the Pit;**
>
> **Proverbs 1:13   We shall find all kinds of precious possessions, We shall fill our houses with spoil;**
>
> **Proverbs 1:14   Cast in your lot among us,**
>
> **Let us all have one purse"**—

Greed drives the gang member. Verse thirteen points out that the members are only interested in gaining wealth by taking from others. They use their intellect, their energy and all their time, plotting another scheme to rob their unsuspecting victims. Gang members want "all kinds of precious possessions", and they want to "fill our houses with the spoil". The problem with their plan is that the only road they want to take to achieve their prosperity is by "swallowing" their victims alive! This is the way the victims will feel after an encounter with gang-bangers. I have been a crime victim and I did, at that time, feel violated beyond definition! With the fear and anger that the crime instilled in me, I felt as if I was being swallowed alive and that I ended up in hell!

In the recruiting process, gang members will tell new and potential recruits to come and join them so that they all will have "one purse". Recruiters indicate that the wealth that will be obtained by the gang will be shared by all members and that each member will have his piece of the pie. The truth of the matter, however, is not so pleasant. Once a person joins the gang, he or she will find that he has no power. He is there to do and perform the will of those gang members who have been in the gang longer than he has. You are stripped of your right to think and be an individual. You become trapped and you will discover that the only way for you to leave the gang is to become one of the gang's victims. As far as the money and prosperity go, you will soon discover that you, being the new man on the block, are the lowest one on the totem pole. As such, you will find yourself doing all of the work, such as robbing, thieving, mugging, and drug running, and your homeboys will reap the benefits while you take all of the risks. One more thing: I've learned from observation that gang members will not come to visit you while you are locked up in prison! You will find that your fellow gang members were lying about their commitment to be with you through the end.

> **Proverbs 1:15   My son, do not walk in the way with them, Keep your foot from their path;**
>
> **Proverbs 1:16   For their feet run to evil,**
>
> **And they make haste to shed blood.**

To all my African-American brothers, just as this proverb warns and pleads a second time for sons to avoid being a part of those who would want to engage in destructive behavior, I am doing the same. I am making the plea again. The one thing I hear most often in the penitentiary is that the prison gang offers protection. When I ask about the nature of the protection, the answer is always the same. Offenders join one gang in order to protect themselves from members of another gang. What many gang members soon discover is that the price for this false sense of protection is too high, as many of them pay with their lives!

The gang member is further described as one whose "feet run to evil and they make haste to shed blood". In their haste to get what they want, they are willing to do whatever it takes to get it. Young gang members kill people for a joy ride, these days. They shed blood for just the few dollars that a victim may have had on his person. There are too many young African-American brothers on death row and in prison for life, for offenses that netted them less than a hundred dollars. In their haste to obtain wealth, they don't stop long enough to think about the consequences of their actions.

> Proverbs 1:17 Surely, in vain the net is spread in the sight of any bird;
>
> Proverbs 1:18 But they lie in wait for their own blood, they lurk secretly for their own lives.
>
> Proverbs 1:19 So are the ways of everyone who is greedy for gain; It takes away the life of its owners.

Verse seventeen indicates that all of the actions of the gang members is in vain. Even when you set your nets in plain sight of an unsuspecting bird, all of your efforts are in vain. Every time you take a step towards your financial success, you are taking giant steps towards your own failure and demise. This proverb says in verse eighteen that these people are lying in wait for their own blood and they don't realize that they are setting a trap which will cause the end of their own lives. These verses conclude by stating the reality of the end results of gang membership. It says, in essence, that this is the path or the story for anyone who is so greedy for gain and success. They end up losing their lives. In other words, the message to the gang-bangers is, you are committing genocide and you are causing the extinction of our African-American brothers!

For those of you who think you want to be part of a gang, or if you are already a part of a gang, ask yourself the question, "How much have I really gained?" Is the amount you gained worth your life? Even if you have gained masses of wealth, there is a bigger gang-banger with a bigger gun who is willing to set a trap for you in order to take what you have! What do you actually profit by killing and destroying innocent lives in order to obtain a few dollars, especially if you have to eventually repay with your life? How much is your life worth to you? If you are joining the gang for a sense of belonging or for a sense of love and appreciation, there are many other more satisfying ways for you to obtain affection. One way is through the companionship of your African-American sister, you know, the one that you have taken for granted and put on the back burner.

To any would be recruiters, I believe I utter the sentiments of all women in the world when I say, "Stay away from our sons! We don't want them to associate with you. We don't want them to be like you. We don't want our sons to kill or be killed with you or by you. We will do whatever we have to in order to keep them away from you." I have a son and I am going to teach him the proverbs found in the Word of God. I am going to share this book with my son. I am also thankful to God for my husband, my African-American man, who will also teach my son to resist you!

Chapter 7

THE NEW GANG—E.O.A.A.B

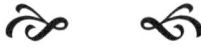

*M*y brothers, you have proven that you have the ability to draw young men to you. You have the ability to train and teach them your ways. They look up to you. They adore you and they want to be just like you. All of this is good! What we need you to do at this point is provide them with the positive roles that they need to follow.

If you want to be a gang member, be a member of the right kind of gang. Start a new gang and a new order! The new gang can be called The Eternal Order of African-American Brothers. Your mission could be to "Rebuild our families and our neighborhoods, one son at a time". Your goal could be met by changing the lives of those closest to you. Begin with your sons and then include your sons' friends. You can change your neighborhoods by getting rid of the gangs and cleaning up the garbage. You can begin by taking care of the children you have fathered. You can begin by staying in school and encouraging your children to do the same.

In the previous chapter, I talked about gangs. The one good thing about gangs is their unity. Although the unity is not unity in the true sense of the word, the gangs still present a false unified front that can be respected. The one thing our African-American brothers must realize is that there is power in unity. There is so much power in unity that unity can change the world! With unity, my African-American brothers, you could bring prison walls down! You wouldn't have to move out of your neighborhoods because you would have the power to change them!

One person working alone would not be effective enough to make a drastic and much needed change. But, if there was a gang of African-American brothers, members of the E.O.A.A.B.; working together, you all would impact every area you stepped into! Afraid of what it would cost? Begin with the small stuff first! What does it cost to pick up trash? What does it cost to paint over graffiti? Clean up the park! Walk children home from school so that they will be safe from predators who come into your neighborhoods and steal your children away from you. Help our sons to read! If you teach them the importance of reading and if they *see* you reading, they will read, too.

The Bible provides us with many examples of the power of unity. In the Book of Genesis, chapter 11, verses 1 through 7, you will find the story commonly called "The Tower of Babel". The story involves a group of people who decided that they were going to build a tower as high as the heavens in order to make themselves equal, so to speak, with God. God was so stirred by their unity, that their effort gained His attention. The thing that intrigues me the most about the incident at the Tower of Babel is the unity of the people.

If you would, look at the scripture. Verses three and four read, "...*Come, let us make bricks;...Come, let us build ourselves a city;...Let us make a name for ourselves.*" These inclusive statements reveal the unity of the people. They identified themselves as one group of people and they identified their purpose and plan. They identified their goal which was to remain united as one people. They realized that they would be stronger if they stayed together and worked together as one people. I've heard it said that the word UNITED could be broken down to effectively mean; U (you) N (and) I – TED (*tied*) together. In order for a group of people to be united, they must have something that ties them together.

Maybe, my African-American brothers, the problem is you all have not been able to identify the thing that will tie you all together! We know for sure that it is not money! Money does more to divide people than it does to bring them together. Money is to people what a fresh kill is to a pack of hungry lions. Animals will fight ruthlessly, maim and kill, just to get a piece of a dead carcass. For the love of money, people will lie fearlessly, cheat and destroy those around them, just to get a few dollars in their possession.

Since it is not money, what is it that will bind all African-American brothers together in harmonious unity? How about our love for our children? How about our love for our people? How about the hope for our future? For the purposes of the new gang, your tie that will bind you together is also your purpose: Eternal Order. Your purpose would be to establish the African-American brothers as a force and voice that will last through the end of this age and to bring order to the chaotic state of our neighborhoods and our people. These are all good things that you could use to bring you all together in unity.

One of my favorite movies is, *The Three Musketeers,* as presented by Richard Lester's film in 1974. In the story, the musketeers were a group of men who were united in their purpose. Their purpose was to protect the king, and in so doing, protect the kingdom. They fulfilled their purpose by putting their motto into action, which was, "All for one and one for all". It was a motto built on the concept of unity. They understood that in order to fulfill their purpose, they had to be united.

The three Musketeers would shout this motto, "All for one and one for all", especially when one member was in trouble and needed the assistance of the other members. The portion of the motto, "all for one", indicated that the group of Musketeers was united in their purpose, to train, to build up, make strong, and protect an individual who was one of their own. Their camaraderie was such that they would even lay down their lives for the sake of the one.

If one was in a battle, they all would fight. If one fell, the rest would do everything to pick him up. My cousins and I are familiar with this philosophy. For the most part, we all grew up together, in close neighborhoods. We played together and we loved each other. Whenever one of us got into trouble, everyone who was available would come to the rescue! We had our differences, but we would put those differences aside when the situation called for it.

The second half of the Musketeer's motto is "one for all". After the training period, this one trainee was then empowered to, in turn, give his whole life for the group. The trainee learned that the needs and power of the whole are far greater than the needs and power of the individual. He has also learned that the goal and purpose of the group, were more important than his individual wants and desires.

For you, my African-American brothers, the motto is more like "all for me and none for you". The idea of sacrificing yourselves for the group, well, you seem to have a problem with that. If one of your brothers was in trouble, instead of sacrificing yourself, you would do whatever you needed to do in order to save yourself. You would lie on your brother or fellow gang member, you would turn your brother in, and you would even run away and hide. If you found yourself in a position where you were going to obtain a large sum of money, you would keep it to yourself and for yourself. If you found yourself in a deep hole of trouble, everyone around you would be in trouble with you because your attitude would be, "If I'm going down, everybody's going down with me".

Through the Three Musketeers film, I established some thoughts regarding the unity that the Musketeers were displaying and practicing. I observed that when a man became a Musketeer, he had to surrender his personality, his beliefs, his own agendas, and his own way of life. His life would no longer be his own, but it would be dedicated to the service of the king. Some of the musketeers left businesses, wealth, family, farms and more, to dedicate themselves to the service of the king. Their first priority was to do the will of the king.

Before you, my African-American brothers, can begin this journey of unity, you have to let go of your differences, which are very minute and insignificant. You are already shrinking in numbers and any division among you would greatly weaken you. How do we get to the point to where we surrender our differences in order to become one? First, you have to identify your purpose. The purpose lives within your hearts. As Christians, our collective purpose is to do the will of the King! As African-Americans, our purpose could simply be the forward movement and progression of our people.

Once we identify what is in our hearts, our next step would be to identify the people we are servicing or helping. This is done by identifying some physical characteristic that solidifies the ties that bind us together. In the story of the Tower of Babel, the people there had the same language. This verbal tie was what separated them from others and it was the strong thing that linked them together. They were able to tell themselves from other groups of people because of their language. As African-Americans, we share the same skin. We share the same history. We have the same ancestors and we can trace our roots back to the same continent.

Another thing that I noted about the Musketeers was the fact that they had uniforms. What does a uniform do? In the same sense as language united the people involved with the Tower of Babel, so does the uniform unite a large group of people into one body. The word uniform can be broken down into two parts. The first part of the word uniform is "uni", which quickly translates to mean "one". The second part of the word uniform is "form". With little imagination, one quickly understands that "form" means "body". The uniform merged and melted the individuals that made up the Musketeers into one body. They were able to tell themselves from other groups by their uniforms. Your uniform, my African-American brothers, is that unique brown skin you were born in. No matter what shade of brown you wear, the uniform, the one body, is the same, as it has its origin in Africa.

Not only do uniforms identify us as being on the same team, the uniform is a picture of strength. The uniform covers differences, hides weaknesses, and is a sense of protection. When people see the uniform and realize that you are not by yourself, they automatically recognize the strength in your numbers. The uniform makes us feel like we belong, that we are part of the family, so to speak. Gang members understand this concept, but they use the positive thing for something negative.

The United States military is another example of this philosophy. Growing up, I was a military child, traveling to different countries and different parts of the United States to my stepfather's next duty assignment. His last assignment before he retired from the army was Fort Hood, Texas. I remember the marching and the chanting that the soldiers would do every morning. Their synchronized marching was the picture of strength and power. Their uniformity was a sight to see! You couldn't help but be impressed by the sheer number of men all marching together, in the same direction, to the same rhythm, in precise formation, under the instructions of one cadence caller. You immediately understood the unspoken rule that if you messed with one of the soldiers, you were going to have to face them all.

A person who was new to the military scene would probably wonder how did all of these men from different backgrounds, from all walks of life, different cultures, different ethnicities, and different histories, come together to form such a great vision of power and force. Listening to my stepfather's stories, I understood how all of the individual men came together to form one legion.

It begins in basic training where the men, from all walks of life, make a choice to come together for one purpose, and that is to protect the kingdom—the USA—at all cost. On the first day of basic training, individuals are stripped of their individuality. Their heads are shaved and their civilian clothes are exchanged for military uniforms. Regardless of the financial status of their families, they are given the same bedding, and they sleep in the same quarters. They are all treated the same. They are all taught that they will defend the country by defending each other. They learn that everyone and everything that everyone does is equally important. Each individual quickly realizes he is part of something that is greater than he is.

I remember vividly, during the initiation of Desert Storm. Ordinarily, driving through Fort Hood, one would be overwhelmed by a sea of drab green. Everything was green or a shade of green or green camouflage. From the tanks, to the buildings, to the warehouses to the officers' uniforms themselves, everything was green! It seems to me, that when the United States became involved in Desert Storm, everything went from drab green to desert-sand tan and beige camouflage in the matter of a few days! The united change occurred so quickly that you would have thought it happened overnight! That's what I call teamwork, togetherness and unity! When one made the change, they all made the change.

My African-American brothers, you too can attain a position in this country that will cause others to look at you and take notice of your oneness, and they will be able to see the potential power that your togetherness represents! Currently, in your discombobulated state, you all are running around in different directions, seeking your own success, by yourself, for yourself, with no regard to anyone else.

You may be asking yourself, "Why is it so important to be a part of the team, the E.O.A.A.B.?" The answer to that is simple. If you have ever played sports you know the importance, first of all, of the uniform. You didn't really feel like you belonged on the team until you received your uniform. You may not have been able to play a lick, but when you received your uniform, you felt stronger, you walked differently with your uniform on, and you had pride. You knew that everywhere you went, people would recognize you as part of the team. You had pride and you didn't want to do anything to embarrass the team.

Guess what! Whether we like it or not, people put all African-Americans on the same team. Everyone else thinks that African-Americans ought to be able to answer all of the questions to the dilemmas surrounding our African-American people. Others think that we should know why our brothers commit so many criminal offenses. Others think we all should know why so many of our young girls are getting pregnant before they learn how to drive. Others think we should know why so many of our children are dropping out of school. Since we are all in the same brown skin, we have been identified as being part of the African-American team. To a certain degree, I agree with everyone else. That is why I am sending out this message. Our team is suffering and we are the only ones who care (or not) and we are the only ones who can rebuild the team and make it stronger.

Unfortunately, instead of being a team player, some of us want to be spectator members. We may want the problem fixed—we may want our team to perform better—but we don't want to do what we need to do in order to make the team better. I remember when my two oldest daughters were in high school. Whenever the Central Jaguars played football, they were there! If it was a home game, they were in the stands, cheering their team. If the game was being played out of town, they would wait anxiously for the team to return home so that they could learn whether or not their team was victorious. The thing that tickled me was on the occasions when the Jaguars lost, instead of my daughters shouting, "*We* won! *We* won!" they would say things like, "*They* lost! Those sorry Jaguars! I told you they were sorry!" Whenever Central played and won, my daughters wanted to be a part of the team. Everybody wants to be part of a winning team. But, whenever Central lost, my daughters would separate themselves from the team. This is the same way many of us treat our African-American brothers and sisters.

Whenever something good is discovered or said about our brothers and sisters, we all want to be a part of the team and claim our African-American heritage. Remember when Tiger Woods wanted to express his Asian heritage? How many of you shouted in objection, "He needs to quit playing! He knows he's black!" I have to admit that I started watching tennis matches when Venus and Serena Williams started playing. I was so excited to see our team expanding its gifts and talents into other areas! Even when O.J. was found not guilty, many of us breathed a sigh of relief!

But then, when the DC sniper turned out to be African-American, I was so embarrassed for our team! Many people of other races were asking me how did I feel and why did I think he did it! Others felt that I should have known the answers to their questions because he was on my team! I know many of you went through the same thing. No matter what we think, no matter how wealthy we get, no matter how far from the ghetto we go, we can't escape our team, because this brown skin that we are in is our uniform and it will follow us to our grave, even if we try to dye it white!

This uniformity of our African-American heritage should be the tie that binds us together instead of the thing that separates us. We have divided ourselves into sub-colors—light brights, yellow bone, chocolate, brown, tan, dark, black, and everything else. Our skin tone is our heritage and we should wear it proudly. Instead of dividing along lines defined by the hue of our skin, we should just put all of the browns in one pot and be on the same team. The uniformity hides our differences, protects our weaknesses, and gives us a sense of belonging. It is the picture of strength, and it makes us one. When we all come to realize that we are on the same team, we will walk differently and our pride in being part of the team will help to keep us from doing things to embarrass the team.

This uniform helps us to recognize who our real enemy is. Too many of us come to the playing field without our uniform on and we end up playing against each other, failing to recognize we are on the same team. We are not supposed to be playing against each other. Neither does it do us any good to talk down to the members of our team. We should be building each other up. We are to be playing against the other team! The enemies, as far as African-Americans, are concerned are illiteracy, teen pregnancy, the drastic rise of HIV and AIDS among our people, the increase of drug sales and drug use in our neighborhoods, gang violence, poverty, black on black crimes and joblessness, to name a few.

The reason we need to come together is because unity brings about results. Unity is power and strength. Where one person can't do it alone, together, we can make a difference. In the spiritual sense, unity gets God's attention! If you look back at the story of the Tower of Babel, you will read in verses five through seven that God was concerned about the unity of the people. Their unity was so powerful that God responded by saying, (Genesis 11:6) *And the LORD said, "Indeed the people are one and they all have one language, and this is what they begin to do; now nothing that they propose to do will be withheld from them."* God recognized that a unified people will be able to do whatever they set their minds to do.

This is why our enemies would not want us to come together in unity. Others understand that once we become one, our strength and our power and our voice will increase. In the spiritual sense, Satan does not want husbands and wives to pray together because he knows that their power and strength will increase if they get on one accord. Just as Satan does everything he can to cause division and separation, to keep the two of them from praying together, others try to keep African-Americans from coming together. Well, actually, let me take that back. Others don't have to cause us to be separated because we do a lot of that ourselves. If we can just grasp the concept that in unity there is power, we would be able to change the world, one African-American boy at a time.

Think about this for a moment. Satan knows the power of unity. That's why he is constantly hard at work, trying to divide us. He knows that one crack in a foundation can cause a shift in the whole house. And, just as one person on a row boat, rowing to the beat of his own drum, can throw the forward motion of the boat out of rhythm, one person in the neighborhood selling crack or refusing to comply with the laws of the land, can cause a great upheaval in the community.

Similarly, just as one wrong note can change the melody of a song and it can throw our praise and worship off, so can one unkind word have a detrimental effect on a young person's personality and life. Although it takes unity to build up, it only takes one person sitting down to slow down a parade. One bad apple *can* affect the whole bunch. When you think about gangs and how they started with one person and how that one person infected many people, we realize how easy it is for one person with the wrong agenda and wrong attitude to make a change for the worse.

Another thing that we have to realize is that destruction is easy! There are times when aggressive force is not necessary because in order to destroy something like a dream, all one needs is the small push, the small voice of a negative thought! One negative thought in your mind can keep you from trying to reach your goal! I remember on one occasion when I was speaking to a group of offenders, I asked them what was it that kept them from pursuing their dreams. Almost unanimously, they responded, "the fear of failure". I tried to make them realize that when they failed to try, then their failure was imminent!

I tried to encourage them by letting them know that fear will immobilize their faith. As long as we fear something, we will not try. In order to get over our fear, we have to look at the birth place of our fear. Most often, our fear is born in our minds! There is no tangible reason for us to have the fear, except for the things that we have played over and over in our thoughts and dreams. Nobody has to take anything from us and no one has to sabotage us because we have defeated ourselves in our minds. To overcome the negative things in your mind, focus on the positive! See yourself reaching your goals!

One negative word spoken into the life of a teenager can cause him to feel inferior. Too many times we have been told as African-Americans that we are not as intelligent as people of other races. That is a lie from the pit of hell! All you have to do is study your Black History and see the impact that African-Americans have made in this great nation of ours! There is no reason why African- Americans can't still make an impact on the world outside of the athletic arena.

Let me interject this story. During the summers I was growing up, my brother and I played outside a lot. One year my brother decided that we were going to study insects. Like explorers, we went down the streets of our neighborhood and nearby fields, searching for different bugs. We turned over rocks and dug up red ant beds, in our quest for bugs. After we gathered up the bugs, we drowned them in rubbing alcohol to preserve their integrity. We used large dress maker pins to tack the bugs to a large piece of sheet rock that we salvaged from an abandoned house not too far from our home.

Our fun didn't end there. My brother insisted that we look up each bug in an encyclopedia and we summarized the information on index cards. The cards were taped underneath each insect. Our bug adventure ended only after my mother came home from work and protested our exhibit. Our children still have the ability to be this creative in their thinking and this explorative in their play. They have to get away from the video games and the TV and return to the out doors! Break free from the confines of your mind and dare to dream beyond your wildest imagination! Who knows? Your child may be the next greatest entomologist!

I've seen ex-offenders, high school dropouts, leave the penitentiary with nothing more than a dream and they go on to become very successful, once they have been given the opportunity to expand their thinking! We can begin to break this disease of illiteracy and the feeling of intellectual inferiority by helping and encouraging our children to dream! Don't tell them they can't write a book. Give them paper and pens and encourage them. Don't tell them that scientists aren't black, but instead, give them a microscope and help them to gather up things to study! Don't tell them they can't be doctors. Give them a stethoscope and let them listen to your heart. Don't tell them they can't be singers or actors. Give them a microphone and a stage and teach them to read by using monologues from great plays. Don't tell them they will never be anything. Tell them they can be what ever they want to be!

I know that you have seen on too many occasions where one bad attitude slowed down a project. Remember playing ball with a teammate who had a bad attitude? After you did everything you could to get him to get a better attitude, you wanted to get rid of him when he chose not to change. You didn't want anyone on your team who had a bad attitude, because you knew that the bad attitude would keep the team from moving forward and reaching its goal.

I admonish you to check your attitude in every area of your life. What is your attitude about your job? What is your attitude about your family? What is your attitude about your neighborhood? What is your attitude about your future? Your success begins with your attitude.

In the African-American culture, the church plays a great role. Not only does the church have a positive influence, its influence can be negative if the church is not careful. From one person in the pulpit, to one person in the pew, things that are said and done, in the name of God, can have a negative impact on everyone in the congregation if the church leadership is not careful. That negative impact is then spread throughout the community as members of the church return to their homes.

Churches should be houses of refuge but some of them have turned out to be houses of pain and shame. Some churches concentrate too much on what a person wears by forcing young girls out of the church for wearing pants. Some churches drag you to the altar, in the name of God, sling oil on you and force you to pray in tongues until you have been delivered from your demon. I have been in churches and I have observed how people will point fingers and curse you in a righteous manner, telling you how unholy you are and that you are going to hell. They condemn you to the point where you feel there is no hope. As Christians, it is our duty and obligation to draw people with the love of Jesus. We can't make people change, only God can. We have to quit condemning people to hell and start opening our arms in love. When we do that, we will draw more people to Christ instead of forcing them into isolation.

As individuals, when we separate ourselves from others and try to live our lives in seclusion, we fail to realize that we can still have an affect on those around us. One lie spoken from our lips can cause the reputation of a good man to turn bad. One person with AIDS can pass his or her infection on to another, and another, and another until an entire community has been impacted. One gangster with a gun can change a family. One absent father can change children. Just as one red sock in the wash can turn the whole load pink, that's the way we can affect people! Even when we try to be loners, we are still a part of the team.

I've learned that with every negative influence there is a positive alternative. With the red sock in the wash, all I would have to do is add just a little bit of bleach and everything the red sock did to destroy, the bleach can fix! So, with everything that individuals have done to destroy our unity, there is a remedy and we can overcome all of the negatives that have been handed to us over the decades. We can begin by changing the words that are coming out of our mouths because these words directly affect the way we think.

The only way to for us to reach our goal is through the display of a united front. We have to make a joint decision to stop referring to each other in the negative and start building each other up. We have to be united within the body, united within our families, united within our neighborhoods and communities, united at our schools, united in our dreams and goals, different organizations united, city, county and states united. We have to be willing to lay aside our differences, our attitudes, our judgmental mentalities, our worldly thinking, our selfishness, our pet peeves, our idiosyncrasies, and the small stuff! Unity is the absence of differences.

There is no room for differences here amongst the African-American community! We need to hang a sign on the front door to our communities saying, "No room for differences here!" There is only one mind, one body, one accord, one mission, one vision – All for one and one for all! We are all African-Americans and we are fighting for the Eternal Order of African-American Brothers!

In order to succeed, we have to adopt the attitude – all for one! When we see some young child fall through the cracks, a drug addict fall, when I fall, when you fall – ALL FOR ONE! We must take the time to raise the one with the same diligence and persistence that the old widow used to retrieve her one lost coin (Luke 15:8, 9)!

Then our attitude should shift to ONE FOR ALL! After you have been lifted, strengthened, built up, empowered, trained, made prosperous, and armored up, then taking on the attitude of Christ, the mind of Christ and be willing to sacrifice yourself for us all. We talk a good game, but when it comes right down to it, are we willing to do what we need to do in order to build someone else up? We have to realize that it's not about you or me as individuals anyway! It's about our sons and our daughters, our families, our culture, and our team! Not only that, but it's about the Gospel, our Lord and Savior Jesus Christ, it's about the kingdom of God, it's about the lost souls.

We can change the world, one individual at a time, as soon as we realize that strong individuals make strong families. Strong families make strong communities. Strong communities make strong cities. Strong cities make strong states, which make our nation strong. Let us not waste anymore time with our own agenda and personal gain. Let's surrender our individual wills for the sake of our brother, for the sake of the E.O.A.A.B. Let us forsake ourselves in order to do the will of God, and unite ourselves with this motto – ALL FOR ONE and ONE FOR ALL, my African-American brothers, for our strength begins with you!

Chapter 8

HOMOSEXUALS, BISEXUALS, METRO-SEXUALS AND D.L.'S

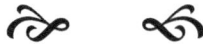

When talking about genocide or self-annihilation or self-destruction, my exposé would not be complete if I didn't address this particular method of self-extermination. Now, fellas, before you close the book and turn me off, know that I am not judging you. I love you! You are my brother and I am your keeper.

The point is, engaging in same-sex sexual activity greatly increases your risk of contracting HIV which causes AIDS. And, the bottom line, regarding HIV and AIDS is that it is a life threatening disease for which there is no cure! As J. L. King pointed out in his book, *"On the Down Low"* (2003), more and more of you strong African-American brothers are engaging in sexual activity with each other! Not only are you killing each other, but you are killing us and your children too! When you are infected with the AIDS virus, you transmit the disease to your unsuspecting female partners, because you hide the fact that you are having homosexual relationships. You even try to water down the fact that you are homosexual by refusing to call yourself a homosexual! Okay, I can deal with that. I will refer to your behavior the same way you do, by calling it same-sex sexual behavior. But, no matter what you call it, this type of sexual behavior is life-threatening and your eagerness to participate in this type of self-annihilation is insanity to the tenth power!

The reason I identify this behavior as being genocide, is because this is destructive behavior that causes death. Like other destructive behavior such as drug use, alcoholism, and cigarette smoking, homosexuality or same-sex sexual activity has a negative effect on your life's span. Likewise, just as your loved ones would want to convince you to stop using alcohol or drugs, your loved ones would want you to stop same-sex sexual activity. Just as alcoholism and drug addiction has negative effects on families, so does this abnormal lifestyle.

I have heard too many times that the tendency to be homosexual is something that some individuals were born with and it is something that they just can't resist and can't help. I have also heard these same confessions from the incarcerated offenders I have interviewed and had conversations with. In one aspect, I agree. As the Word of God points out in the seventh and eighth chapters of Romans, as long as we are in the *flesh*, we have a tendency to *sin*. Sin can easily be defined as anything that contradicts the will and Word of God. Although I believe that there *may* be some chemical imbalances in one's body that would cause him or her to be an alcoholic, but what I also believe that no one forces you to take a drink! You make the conscious decision whether or not you want to drink alcohol and, with all of the ad campaigns regarding the overindulgence of alcohol consumption, and alcoholism awareness, you can't use the excuse that you didn't know!

Too many people use the inborn defense as an excuse or they will say things like, "I couldn't help myself", or "my desire was so strong that I couldn't resist". If we say that a certain inborn nature that leads to unacceptable behavior is a *disease* and not a matter of choice, then we are saying that the actor is the victim of his own unnatural instincts and all of his unnatural behavior would have to be justified and excused as something that he couldn't help. That means when pedophiles commit their offenses and claim that it was their nature, we would have to excuse their behavior as instinctive. The same would hold true for people who claim that they are *born* alcoholics when they end up killing innocent people. Their behavior would have to be excused because of their claim of some genetic default. Where would we draw the line?

There is one thing that I will agree with. As creatures of our flesh, we have this *inborn* nature to sin. For example, no one has to teach a two-year-old how to lie. I have five children and each one of them has been two years of age at one point in their lives. There have been too many occasions where one of my children was caught doing something wrong, and when asked, the child would say, "not me!" If I found something that was broken and asked how it got that way, each one of my children would provide me with a different story. We don't teach our children to lie, but when they learn the negative consequences of their behavior, they will lie in order to avoid being punished. They will lie to avoid your chastisements. And, sometimes, they will go so far as to justify their behavior.

As Christians and as humans with intellect and the freewill ability to choose, we have to constantly fight against the desires of our flesh especially when those desires are *sinful*, plain and simple. I cannot judge my homosexual, bisexual, metro-sexual or my down low African-American brothers. The Bible tells me in I John 1:8, that if I *"say that (I) have no sin, (I) deceive (myself) and the truth is not in (me)"*. To judge someone would imply that I am without sin and I have a righteous conscience that would be able to separate sinful behavior from non-sinful behavior. The only measuring stick that I have to gauge my behaviors as good or bad, sinful or righteous, is the Bible. The only thing that I am doing, in this chapter and in this book, my African-American brothers, is bringing you to a greater awareness of behavior that is sinful according to God's standards, not mine. What I am supposed to do is identify what God's Word says, then you and I as individuals should gauge our behavior to see how it lines up with God's Word. If I see that my behavior is sinful, what I am supposed to do is confess my sins so that God will forgive me.

There are many times, on a daily basis, that we all make decisions as to whether or not we are going to do God's will or go against it. From lying, to stealing, to committing adultery, to murdering someone, we make choices all the time. The example that I shared about the lying two-year-olds is just the beginning. As adults, we constantly face situations where we have to decide whether we are going to lie or tell the truth. Think about the last time you were late for work. Did you tell the truth about your tardiness?

Not only do we lie, but we justify our behavior. A thief would say that the only reason he stole some food was because he was hungry and needed something to eat. The thief would feel justified in his reasoning because we all would agree that no one should go hungry. What we have to do is take it a step further. No one should go hungry, so every neighborhood should be able to provide assistance to those who may be in dire need of food. I am sure that there are services, agencies, churches and neighbors who are available and who would be willing to assist the hungry person and eliminate the need for him or her to steal.

My African-American brothers, you take your justifications to another level. You justify your behavior, saying that "that's just the way I am". Well, I beg to differ. That's just the way you *choose* to be! Everyday we wake up; we decide what type of person we are going to be. Think about the use of the *inborn* defense for homosexuals and for homosexual behavior. The problem with the inborn defense supporting same-sex sexual activity is that it removes responsibility from the actor and he (or she) does not have to confess a sin or activity that he feels he cannot control. The bottom line is, the decision to engage or not engage in sexual activity is a self-made decision—it is a conscious choice. The only way to be forgiven of a sin is to confess it. Satan does not want you to confess your sin, so he has given you this false sense of security in your claim that you have no control over your behavior.

The truth, whole truth, and nothing but the truth, please! We have been given the freedom of choice! Maturity, wisdom and freewill have the power to override inborn-tendencies! A two-year-old will exhibit self-survival skills and the inborn nature to put self first. This is exhibited in the two-year-old's habit of calling everything, "mine". A two year old will bite, hit, and scratch in order to protect or defend himself. No one has to teach a two year old how to throw a temper tantrum in order to get his way.

However, as the two year old matures and increases in wisdom, he learns alternate behavior that is more appropriate and acceptable. Nevertheless, although he has matured, he still has to make the conscious decision between his instincts or learned behavior and more acceptable behavior.

In nearly everything we do, we go through a mental course of action during the decision making process. Even though breathing is an inborn, natural act, I can still decide to hold my breath. As a matter of fact, I can hold my breath for so long that I pass out! Fortunately, when I pass out, nature will take over and I will start to breathe again. Although breathing is something in my life that I can't live without, there is a lot in my life that I can.

Another inborn tendency or natural desire is sex. God created us to be sexual creatures. He would not tell us to "be fruitful and multiply and replenish the earth", (Genesis 1:28), and then not give us the desire we would need in order to fulfill His command. Sexual desire may be inborn and instinctive to a degree, nevertheless, we have the ability to control our pursuance to fulfill our urges, we have the ability to control our sexual conduct. As with several other instinctive and inborn behaviors such as eating and sleeping, we still have the intellectual ability to control what we do. We still choose who, what, how much, where and when concerning our sexual behavior.

Remember how appalled you were when the stories about Catholic priests molesting young boys came out? I have learned that Catholic priests are not the only ones who are seducing young boys into homosexual behavior. I know for a fact that old white men are not the only ones preying on young boys and forcing them into acts of sodomy. There are also deacons, preachers and elders in the black church who are seducing young black boys into the undercover world of sexual perversion. From my many conversations with you, my African-American brothers, I am aware that you take our young fatherless boys and drag them into your sexual underworld by pretending you want to be a father figure to them. I know that you seduce them with video games, camping trips, trips to amusement parks, money, and companionship. You take them in, pretending to love them, then you sodomize them, ruining them for the rest of their lives!

It has become painfully clear to me that many of you do what you do to young boys because someone else did it to you when you were a boy. Again, I have had many conversations with offenders who identified themselves as being homosexual or bisexual. Many of them, the majority of them in fact, indicated that they were raped, sodomized and/or molested when they were boys. Many of them never got over the trauma that the crime against them caused. There were a few who said they'd been raped during prior incarcerations. Nevertheless, instead of using your past, as reasons to engage in sexually immoral behavior in your present, use the pain that you felt as a result of your past as reason to protect those you would otherwise harm. Just because somebody violated you doesn't give you the right to violate somebody else.

There were also many offenders that I have had conversations with who indicated that they were not homosexual, but that they were real men who had sex with other real men while in the penitentiary. They indicated that when they were released, they were going back home to their wives or girlfriends. There were a few of the offenders that I spoke with who admitted to participating in same-sex sexual activity simply out of "curiosity".

More and more, African-American men are participating in same-sex sexual activity. And, if the truth be told, many of these practitioners are coming out of our churches! These dirty old and young men see the emptiness in the faces of fatherless boys in the church. You put your arms around the young boys, pretending to offer them the love that they have longed for. You tell their mothers that you want to teach them a thing or two about life. Their mothers, worn out from the battle to rear their sons in the admonition of the Lord, are grateful for the helping hand that you have extended to them. After you have gained everyone's confidence, you take advantage of our sons behind our backs, but at the same time, right in front of our faces!

One story that painfully comes to my mind is the story of Corey, a boy in my friend's church. Corey's mother had her hands full with her three daughters and two sons. Of course, all of the children had different fathers and neither of the fathers was around to help Corey's mother raise them. Corey was the middle child and he was the most difficult to handle. He was hard to handle in school, and he was even more difficult to handle in church. When speaking to him about his behavior, many of the adults in church would just chastise him and never take the time to reach beneath his hard exterior to discover what was really paining him to the point where he acted out.

Mr. Ed, one of the deacons and a junior high school teacher, took an interest in Corey. He started taking control of Corey whenever he became uncontrollable at church. Since he taught at the same school where Corey was a student, Mr. Ed took an interest in Corey's school activities and classes as well. Soon, with all of the care and concern that Mr. Ed was showing Corey, Corey began to make changes for the better. His behavior and his grades improved.

Corey liked Mr. Ed and enjoyed being with him, but he was still suspicious about some of Mr. Ed's behavior. When Corey asked his mother about the possibility of Mr. Ed being gay, Corey's mother quickly put aside Corey's fears, explaining that Mr. Ed is a "ladies man" and he knows all of the right things to say and all of the right things to do for a woman. Although Corey still had his reservations, he continued to allow Mr. Ed to be the father figure in his life.

One day, the unthinkable happened. Mr. Ed asked Corey's mother if Corey could spend the weekend with him. Mr. Ed asked this of Corey's mother without asking Corey first. Corey's mother, who was pleased with Corey's progress, agreed that the weekend with a real man was just the thing that Corey needed. When Corey learned about the weekend getaway, remembering his reservations, he protested, but his protests were in vain. As added protection, Corey asked if his friend Peewee could join them. After a few minutes of debate, Mr. Ed agreed to let Peewee join them for the weekend.

The weekend progressed nicely. Mr. Ed took the boys out for pizzas and a movie, something that Corey's mother did not have the opportunity to do. He took the boys back to his apartment and they watched videos. During the last movie, Mr. Ed made a pallet on the floor for Peewee and said that Corey was going to sleep with him. Corey felt nervous anxiety rising up in him and insisted that he should sleep on the floor in the living room, with Peewee.

Mr. Ed's strong conversation led Corey to believe that he was going to do something to Corey if he did not sleep in the bed with Mr. Ed. Finally, when it was time for bed, Mr. Ed left the television on for Peewee, explaining that he set the timer for an hour. He led Corey to his bedroom and locked the door behind him. It did not take long before Mr. Ed was making sexual comments and advances towards Corey, while he was caressing Corey's young body and removing his clothes.

What Mr. Ed failed to realize was that Corey came prepared. He struggled and managed to break free from Mr. Ed's grip. He ran to his backpack and withdrew the pistol that he was carrying. He'd gotten the gun from Peewee's house. It was a gun that belonged to Peewee's mother. When Mr. Ed advanced towards Corey, Corey spun around, with the gun in his hands, pointed it at Mr. Ed's chest, closed his eyes and pulled the trigger. Mr. Ed fell to his knees.

This is not the end of the story. Although Corey merely defended himself, he was arrested for Voluntary Manslaughter with a Deadly Weapon, which was reduced from a murder charge. Throughout the police investigation, no one could say that Mr. Ed was a homosexual. No one would testify to the fact that Mr. Ed had allowed many other boys to spend the night at his apartment, before Corey. No one, not at the church or at the school, had anything bad to say about Mr. Ed. Not even Peewee, the closest one to the incident other than the victim and the perpetrator, could provide investigators with any information that would have helped them identify which person in the incident was actually the victim.

Corey, on the other hand, had many incidents of violence on his record. Many people advised investigating officers that Corey had a temper and that he acted out often. No one could explain why Corey would want to hurt such a *nice* man who did everything for the boys in the neighborhood. No one believed Corey's story. No one believed that Mr. Ed was a child molester because he kept his behavior and activities secret and hidden. He was also able to keep his victims silent, even after his death.

Although the names have been changed and the situation modified to protect the identities of those involved, this is a real incident. Corey was about fourteen years of age when the incident happened and he ended up going to prison. At the time of this printing, he was released to a halfway house after serving several years in prison. He is currently in his twenties.

I have observed on several different talk shows, that a new trend has been developing. Men who are married and have children come out of the closet and say they are homosexual. Some have even gone through sex change operations. Their defense for their behavior, for the most part, is that their desire to be a woman, or to be homosexual, is something they were born with and they just couldn't help it. Here again, we are intellectual beings with the freedom of free will! We can decide not to engage in a particular behavior, regardless of the desire to do it!

For example, the women who are married to these men and choose to stay with them make the choice to do so. Some of them remain celibate because they don't want to cheat on their husbands and they don't want to be infected with the HIV that their husbands may be carrying. These women exercise strength and restraint by suppressing their own sexual desires. These women put aside their own dreams for the sake of the family and in support of their husbands. The sacrificial attitude of these women is something that should have been exercised by the men in these situations. Just because you may *want* to do something, doesn't mean you *have* to do it! When you get right down to it, the bottom line is that we are in control of our actions!

We make conscious decisions daily. Sometimes our actions

become so routine that we make decisions regarding them without a whole lot of mental dialogue. At that point, when our activities become routine and second nature, they become habits. If you have ever tried to get a thumb-sucker to stop sucking his thumb, you know that old habits are hard to break!

When you get to the point where your behavior is habitual, you find yourself indulging in your desires simply because you want to. You get to the point where your behavior becomes natural to you and you participate in the behavior with little or no mental interference, and with little or no remorse. It's like the mornings when I drive myself to work. Driving the same road everyday, five days a week, fifty-two weeks a year, my behavior becomes so routine and habitual that I don't have to have a mental discussion about which roads to take. Soon, I find myself pulling into the parking lot of my place of employment and I can't remember any specific details about the journey. That's how destructive behavior eventually gets. You've done it so long and so often until you don't really remember doing it.

If you are involved in harmful behavior and that behavior has become so much a part of you that it is a mindless, thoughtless habit, you have to unlearn that behavior before you can begin to overcome it. For some of you, you have been engaging in your self-destructive behavior for so long that the only way for you to break free is to be delivered.

There is a difference between being rescued and being delivered. When you are rescued, you are taken out of your situation and your mess. Your rescuer, such as your mother, your wife, your sister, or your brother, ends up doing all of the work and you don't have to do anything. You don't even have to say whether or not you want to be taken out of your situation.

Your rescuer will see that you are in danger and because she loves you so much, she will be willing to risk her life for you. If you were not ready for the change that was forced upon you, all you have to do is wait around until your rescuer gets tired of watching you and you can go right back to your old habits. Rescuing can occur and there is no change in the person being rescued.

The rescue gives you the false sense of security. But realize that just because you have been rescued, the fight is not over! Your enemy—which is the thing that you need to be delivered from—will pursue you. If your enemy pursues you and overtakes you, you will still be in a state of confusion and entrapment and you will be trying to break free of your past and at the same time trying to continue to fulfill your desires in secret! This would be the worst position for you to be in because you would think that you were safe and on your way to heaven but the truth is; you would still be lost and on your way to hell!

Wants and desires that fuel drug addiction, alcoholism, and homosexuality get to the point where they overpower our common sense. Reality becomes distorted. When you have reached that point in your life, you need supernatural intervention in order to be set free.

When you are delivered, a change happens! First of all, deliverance is the result of your desire to change! If you don't want to change, there is nothing your family can do and there is nothing that God *will* do in order to help you. Your rescue occurs on the surface and is only temporary. In order to be delivered, you have to be willing to accept the change that will occur *in* you. In order to be delivered, you have to be willing to take off your old self and be ready to put on a *new* self! Being rescued only takes you out of your mess but being delivered takes your mess out of you! If you really want to be delivered from your sexual immorality (or drug addiction, or the pains of your past, or whatever) email me at: iwant2bdelivered@ragenterprise.com.

As I advised you in previous chapters, I am advising you in this one. I am going to do everything that I can to warn young men about your homosexual tendencies. Not only am I going to share this book with my son, but I am also going to share it with his friends. We will talk about sex. We will talk about sexual immorality. We will talk about abstinence and celibacy. We will discuss the fact that predators come in all shapes, colors, and sizes. Predators come from many different backgrounds. He will know that some predators are married and have children of their own. I will do everything that I can to ensure that my son and his friends are well informed. To be sure, I am also going to warn my daughters about you as well. Nobody, and I do mean *nobody* wants to be infected with the AIDS virus and nobody wants to be affected by your deviant sexual behavior.

Just remember, my African-American brothers, we are not judging you. We are addressing your behavior because it is threatening your lives and ours. When you engage in sexually immoral behavior in secret, contract HIV, and bring the disease home to me, you commit the same murderous act as if you put your hands around my throat and watched as you slowly squeeze my life from me. We want you to stop, not because we are judging you, but because you are killing yourselves slowly and we want you to stop dying needlessly! We love you and we want you to love us in return.

Chapter 9

RECOGNIZE YOUR POWER

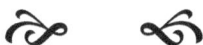

☙ ❧

*T*o my African-American brothers, it is time for you to recognize your power! You already dominate in football and basketball. You even have a strong representation in baseball. You are greatly represented in track and field events. You have tennis shoes named after you that everybody, regardless of race, wants. Remember when everybody wanted "to be like Mike?" Name another sports figure of any other race that had that type of drawing power. Fellas, everyone recognizes your power but you.

Just imagine. If you have the ability to excel in everything, what would happen if you expanded your areas of expertise to other athletic arenas? What about tennis? Venus and Serena have already inspired many African-American girls and boys to explore this field of ball play. Golf anyone? Tiger Woods has set a new standard! Yes, I know he has a mother of Asian decent, but it was his African-American father who recognized his potential and took the time to train him in order to ensure that he would reach his full potential.

Brothers, I challenge you. Is there a swimming pool in your area? If there is, take advantage of the opportunity to learn how to swim correctly. Use the energy you expend doing nothing or the energy you use to commit criminal offenses to learning a new pastime. If there is no pool in your area, check the phone book for the nearest gym, YMCA or college campus, which may have a pool where you can learn new skills. If you learn the skills and practice, I am sure that you will dominate and make your name in the area of your choosing.

Not only is there swimming, but there is also skiing, hockey, soccer, horse jockeying, bowling, archery, mountain climbing and so much more! You can succeed and excel in everything you do. Others already recognize your power and potential. It's time for you to recognize it for yourself. Instead of turning your power into rage and inflicting harm on each other, release that energy into more positive arenas and reach your potential.

I understand that many of you work so hard at excelling in sports because you have been told for many years that you were genetically built for it. You have been told that your strong backs and your long legs help you to jump higher, run faster and hit harder. I beg to differ. The reason you all succeed in sports, such as football, basketball, boxing and track, is because you practice and you work at it! Someone put a basketball in your hands when you were two years old. Someone gave you a drum set when you were three. You started swinging a bat when you were four. You have been running since you learned how to walk, and you have been singing since you learned how to talk. You think about basketball in the morning and all day long, until you can get to the court and work on everything you have been thinking about. Basketball is your life, your dream, and for many of you, it is your ticket out of the ghetto! The reasons you excel in basketball and football is the same reasons why Venus and Serena excel in tennis, and Tiger excels in golf. Those reasons are practice, dedication, perseverance, endurance, motivation and determination. The only problem that I have with your early start in sports is the fact that too many times we focus on the sport and we forget to teach you how to read and write!

Additionally, the reason I disagree with the notion that African-Americans are genetically built for sports is simple. As African-Americans, our lineage has been so scrambled with people of different races and ethnic backgrounds that we can't simply call ourselves "African", because we are not purely African! We call ourselves African-American because we recognize that we have African ancestors, but we also recognize that we, as individuals, represent the "melting pot" notion associated with the United States. Only some few short generations ago, my African-ism was mixed with Caucasians, American Indians and only God knows who else! When you get right down to it, I can't blame my athletic ability on my African ancestry alone because I am only a watered down African, at best!

Not only that, but if basketball is a "black" thing as some have been saying, then all blacks would be able to play basketball. The same thing goes with tap dancing, football, singing, rapping, and dancing. I've seen many black males, over six feet tall, who could not, and I do mean, absolutely, could not play basketball! There are many blacks who can't dance because they have no rhythm. There are many blacks who can't sing because they can't hold a note in a bucket, even if I cut it off of a piece of sheet music for them and put it in the bucket myself! Black boys and girls who grow up in white neighborhoods tend to act "white", whatever that means. At any rate, not all of us excel in sports. For those of us who don't, we have to find another dream to pursue in order to make ours come true!

We often attribute genetics towards our abilities to do certain things. More often than not, it is not genetics that cause our success, but our success comes because of the training that begins at an early age. Remember when the Romanians dominated in gymnastics? At another point and time in history, Americans made strong appearances—due to training, not genetics! Kenyans have long been identified as great distance runners. In my opinion, it is not because they have the genetic make up to be great distance runners, but it is the fact that they have the jungles and mountains in their backyard that they can use as a training ground and they practice running great distances, starting at an early age! Historically, Asians have dominated in the area of martial arts, but as more and more of us are beginning to train with the great masters of the art, more and more people, of all backgrounds, are making strong appearances in the sport.

When you get right down to it, it's not what you are born with, but it's what you *do* with what you're born with and what you do with what you are given! For example, you could be a natural born genius, but if you never act upon your ingenuity, what is your genius worth? With this thought in mind, one would begin to understand how history keeps having these "exceptions" to the rules. Ordinary people take what they are born with and they take the opportunities they are given, and they exercise what they have in order to reach their desired goal. This is how a man who is 5 feet 11 inches can dunk a basketball as well as, if not better than, one who is 6 feet 4 inches tall. This is also why African-Americans, male and female alike, tend to fall short in the academic arena. We were born with the same intellectual abilities as everyone else, but we don't focus or pursue academia. We don't take the intelligence we were born with and exercise it in order to reach our full potential, intellectually speaking. Too many times, we allow our intelligence to hibernate and we settle for the things that come easiest to us.

Let me move on. In addition to sports, you excel in the area of music. Every time you start a new music style or trend, you set a new standard. You started out singing spirituals in the cotton fields to ease the heaviness of your burdens. Then you moved up to scatting and singing the blues. Soon, others learned your craft and mimicked you. Later on, you started singing rock and roll. Others took your music, put their faces on it and sold it as their own. But that didn't stop you! You kept producing more rock and roll and soon others had to realize that they did not have the ability to keep up with you. They didn't have the ability to take away or keep your influence hidden.

Additionally, you sang Gospel and you dominated in that area. Your name and music can now be found in our Baptist Hymnals. Your Gospel music is being sung by people of all races and denominations. People of all nations want to experience a concert featuring you because they recognize the powerful gift that is in you.

The thing that you need to realize is that when you started playing music, you did not have the opportunity to attend the music schools that were in existence. You did not have a formal teacher, so, you became your own teacher. All someone had to do was put a guitar in your hands and give you a few minutes and you were playing not only the traditional chords you heard, but you also stepped outside of the box and began playing in ways that were never heard of. The same holds true for you and the piano, for you and the sax, and for you and the trumpet. I have seen you take overturned buckets and two broken pieces from a broom stick and beat out a hypnotic rhythm that would cause passersby to pause and take in your musical gift.

My African-American brothers, you started singing R&B and hip hop and you have dominated. You started rapping and you dominated. I cant' help but say it again. God has given you the opportunity to dominate in whatever you make up in your mind that you want to accomplish. Everybody recognizes your power and your influence but you!

To emphasize my point, let me share this true story with you. I was driving down a busy roadway one day when I came to a traffic light and I had to stop at the intersection. I could hear your rap music bumping and thumping loudly in a vehicle that was coming up alongside me. The firecracker red sports car with its chrome grill and darkly tinted windows inched its way towards the light. As the car approached the intersection in the lane next to me, I caught a glimpse of the spinners on the rims that were glistening in the sun.

My curiosity got the best of me so I kept my attention on the car and hoped that the light would not change too soon. I wanted to catch a glimpse of the African-American brother who was in the driver's seat. As the vehicle continued forward, I let out a breath when I saw that the window was down. When I came face to face with the driver, I had to smile. There in the car was a young Asian male, wearing his cap to the side. I smiled at him and he returned the gesture. I had to hold back my laughter when the young man's smile revealed a silver studded grill!

Your musical influence has crossed racial barriers and it has been felt for decades. Back in the day, you sang love ballads that have made many weddings and marriages more memorable. Your deep sultry voice has this hypnotic appeal that captures and holds our attention. We have listened with great pride knowing that the words of the love ballads express the deep love that only an African-American brother has the courage to feel.

Presently, it pains us deeply as we open our ears and our eyes to the realization that the love ballads are fewer and further between. Songs like those that were sung by the great balladeers are in our past. We listen but we can't hear your voice singing of your undying love for us in our ears. We search but can't find an African-American brother who will express his love for us, and to us.

Your love songs have been replaced with songs of hatred, not only for authority, but for us as well. You sing about everything you want to do *to* us, but you don't sing anymore about what you want to do *for* us. We have been reduced from queens, princesses, wives, sisters and lovers to b--tches, hoochies, wenches, "ho's" and baby mommas, and you sing songs about your ability to buy us for a dime.

The sad thing about that is; many African-American women have accepted your demotion! We think it is a good thing to be a "hoochie" from the ghetto. Since all you seem to want from us is our bodies for a minute, we show you more and more of what we have to offer! Many young women walk around with too much makeup on their faces, too much fake hair glued onto their heads, and too little clothing on their bodies just to get your attention! We have learned how to "shake that thang" and "back that thang up," and we do everything to make our derrière "bootylicious". It is as if we have lowered our own standards to match your degradation of us and we want you to look at our bodies with lust and not care about our minds. What the young women fail to realize is that after you take their bodies, you don't want anything else to do with them, even if they come back to you later and say they are pregnant with your child!

You no longer sing the songs about loving us forever. Those have been replaced with songs of abuse and one night stands. You sing songs about taking us for granted and taking advantage of us. You sing about how easy it is for you to have your way with us. We just want things to be the way they were. We just want to be loved.

You keep singing these songs that present us in a negative light and the world keeps taking it in. You have set the trend and many are following after you. It saddens me to think that you are gaining your wealth and fame by degrading and insulting me. What saddens me even more is the fact that after you have used us for your promotions, you leave us in the ghetto, to raise your children by ourselves because you think we are nothing but gold diggers.

Initially I thought your songs were only a poetic expression and did not represent your true feelings. However, my thoughts changed and reality set in as the more you found your success down the road of a rapper, the more your actions towards us were letting us know how you really feel about us. One day, young African-American women are going to realize that when they pay their hard earned money to attend one of your concerts and all you do is talk bad about them and to them, they will awaken from their deaf sleep and realize their true worth. At that fateful moment, you will look up and they will be gone. Success is nothing if you have no one to share it with.

Not only is your powerful originality expressed and presented in the music you sing, but it is also present in the music you play. Your drums have more rhythm. Your bass guitar has more thump and your lead guitar has more strings, chords and runs. Your saxophone has more soul and your keyboards just have more of everything. Everyday, more and more people are trying to imitate the style and nature of your music. What they fail to understand is that your music is a part of you and it comes from within you. Not because you were *born* with it, but you grew up with it. It has been a part of your culture for many generations. And, you have perfected your distinctive and original sound. Your style may be often imitated, but it is never, ever duplicated.

Even in the way you dress and wear your hair, you set a trend that others try to make their own. Remember when you were wearing your big natural afros? How many of our racial counterparts applied curly perms to their long straight hair, just to get the look you were born with? Even today, your brothers of other races will go to great lengths to get their hair braided like yours. As dreadlocks are becoming more popular, some have even paid a high price to imitate your natural style in this manner!

You wear your high top fade, they get bowl cuts and taper their sides. You wear one pant leg rolled up, they wear one pant leg rolled up. You wear one glove, so does everyone else. You wear your cap on the side, they do too. You put colored strings in your tennis shoes; it's not long before everyone is doing it. You wear your pants below your buttocks (I don't like this one, but it can't be ignored), they do too! If you would start a new trend where you would wear your pants on your waist with your shirts tucked in, I am sure that your other brothers will do the same.

Not only do you have the ability to dominate in music, sports, and fashion, you also have the potential to make major impacts in the areas of math, science and engineering. There are many African-American brothers who have already made their marks and they have opened up the doors for you to step through and explore your areas of interest. All you have to do is start living and dreaming outside of the confines of your limited imagination.

Don't you realize that the greatest power you have is the power of influence over your sons and daughters? Everyday, they watch you and they imitate you! They grow up to be just like you! Think about all of the times people have expressed to you that you look like your father or that you act just like your father. You may not have known your father, but you have heard people around you talking about him and you have seen pictures of him. You have been influenced by a father you didn't know and your son will do the same. What kind of example are you being for him?

Many times, you can influence your child just by being present. I remember on one occasion when my son was playing football for his junior high school. He did not know that we were going to come to the game that night. Because of my husband's and my hectic and conflicting schedules, we had a very difficult time making it to his midweek scheduled games. That night, as we were walking the long distance from the parking lot to the stands, we could see our son in his defensive position. When the ball was snapped, he halfheartedly fulfilled the responsibility of his position on the field.

We made it to the stands as the team was huddled up near the bench which was close to the stands. My son looked up, just in time to see my husband take his seat. My husband waved at our son and the look on his face immediately changed. After the break, our son trotted out to the field with pep in his step. He aggressively took his place on the line of scrimmage. This time, when the snap took place, my son, with ferocity, pounced across the line and pounded into his opponent with the force of a small rhino! He successfully tackled his opponent who was head and shoulders bigger than he was. His whole mode and tempo of his play changed when he knew that his father was in the stands watching him.

One of my daughters plays basketball with a passion. She is a great team player. She is self-motivated and self-disciplined. She constantly goes to the park near our house where she engages in pick up games with the guys on the court. She plays her heart out whenever she plays, whether her father and I are there or not. However, on the occasions that we are there at the games, my husband, an avid basketball player himself, will coach our daughter from the stands. Because she loves and respects her father and greatly appreciates his presence at her games, she is able to discern his voice over and above everyone else in the gymnasium. She responds to his instructions because of his influence over her.

Just remember, while you are pushing your sons to be the next Michael Jordan or the next Shaq, don't forget that you are their greatest fan and coach, and remember to teach them how to be intelligent men. Remember to remind them of the importance of reading, writing and arithmetic. If you really want to raise up a prince in your son, teach your son to be a gentleman and a gentle man. If your goal is to rear a king, you must teach your son how to love God! Remember, as you are teaching your son, the greatest lessons you could ever teach are the ones you teach by your example!

Chapter 10

RECOGNIZE OUR STRENGTH

❧   ❧

*T*he inner strength of an African-American woman is strength that is to be admired. African-American women have come a long way from the bottom of the totem pole. We start out with strikes against us, the moment we are born. We are African-American, strike one. We are women, strike two. In today's society, if we remain uneducated, that is strike three. The only thing in our lives that we can change is the level of our education. Many of us have stepped up to that challenge.

My mother is the strength in my life. She married my father when she was sixteen and shortly thereafter she gave birth to my brother. After I was born, my mother moved to Fayetteville, North Carolina, with my father, to his newly assigned military post. A few short years later, my mother had the strength to leave my father and return to Oklahoma. She called my grandmother and borrowed money for the train ride home. As soon as she reached Lawton, Oklahoma, she dropped my brother and me off at my grandmother's house and went to find a job. The first thing she wanted to do was pay my grandmother back for the train fare. It didn't take her long to convince a laundry manager to allow her to work for him.

In order for my mother to get to work, my grandfather would drop her off at the bus station early in the morning. She had to wait for the bus in freezing weather and in the rain. After she caught the bus and rode to the other side of town, she still had to walk several blocks to reach her destination. There were many mornings that she arrived at the laundry, too cold to move. Her boss would give her a cup of coffee and allow her to thaw out by the furnace before she had to report to her station. My mother endured because she was determined to take care of her children.

My uncle gave my mother a shack behind his house. He assisted her with putting in the plumbing for a tub, sink and toilet. She put up the sheet rock to turn the one room shack into three parts: bathroom, bedroom and living room/kitchen area.

At that time, she made less than fifty dollars a week but my brother and I always had food to eat. We always had clothes to wear. We always had a roof over our heads. And, we always seemed to have toys under the Christmas tree!

By the time the next winter was about to come, my mother was in a position to purchase a car. She bought the car, even though she could not drive. With the help of my uncle, she was able to get the car home. No one was available to teach her how to drive the car. Everyday, for weeks, armed with nothing but determination, my mother would back the car down the driveway and pull it back up again. Finally, when she was confident in her skills, she drove the car to church, which, at that time, was only a few blocks away from home. By the time the weather was bad again, she had learned to drive the car and she had taken and passed both parts of the driver's examine.

Wherever she went, my mother's priorities would be to get us in school and find a job, wherever she could get a job. She's started out at the entry level, but she has always worked her way up into a supervisory position. She has even gone back to school to take college courses. Today, even though she has retired from a major computer production company, she still works as a substitute teacher. She teaches her students with such authority that many of the school's staff and students think she is a full time teacher!

My grandmother is another picture of strength for me. She ruled with an iron fist! She worked until she just could not work anymore. She taught us the value of a dollar and the taught us the priceless worth of a hard earned dollar. Every paycheck, my grandmother set aside money by placing it into a savings account. Not only was she thrifty, but she also taught us the value of family. Even today, my grandmother still mails out birthday cards to all of her children, grandchildren, great grandchildren and great-great grandchildren.

My aunt is also a strong African-American woman in my life. To survive, she came out of retirement and took on the job as Captain in the Laundry Service Department at a Texas prison. She supervised the laundry staff which included officers and offenders. The unit she was assigned to was capable of housing up to 2897 offenders at one time. On a daily basis, she was responsible for laundering clothes for all of the offenders which included underwear, socks and towels. She was also responsible for laundering officers' uniforms and other clothing belonging to the correctional and non-correctional staff.   She reared her three sons with great discipline and guidance. The three of them went on to become strong African-American Marines who served their country. My aunt also has five successful daughters. Two of them served in the military. My aunt had a hand in bringing up my many other cousins, my brother and me.

When I look back over my life, I remember African-American women like my head-start and kindergarten teachers, Mrs. Kennedy and Mrs. Reese. It is because of them that if I was ever stopped for drunk driving—that wouldn't happen because I don't drink—but if I was ever stopped and instructed to recite my ABC's backwards, I would be able to do that! Mrs. Kennedy and Mrs. Reese are the reasons I behaved in school, all the way through high school! They put a fear in me, at that age, that made me believe something terrible would happen to me if I missed school or if I misbehaved in school!

I do understand that there are occasions where African-American children have had to grow up without the influence of their mother. For whatever reason, maybe your mother was not there. But look into your past and see if you can identify a grandmother, an aunt, an older woman at church or in your neighborhood, or maybe even an older sister. If you look back over your life and you honestly can't see the influence of a strong African-American woman, I apologize to you because you have really missed out. I pray that God will bring a strong African-American woman into your life!

Don't misunderstand me when I say that you need to understand our strength. Just be aware that even though we are strong, we still want to be loved by someone who can be there when we are weak. Our strength is what has kept us through many generations. The more we have been trodden down, the stronger we have become. Over the years, we have learned to continue in our strength, even if we have to do it alone. We have tapped into an inner strength and whatever we are missing, we've learned that God will supply. This message is being written simply because we love you and we just want you to love us in return.

It's been said that the reason African-American brothers turn to women of other races is because the women of other races don't ask questions, and they allow the African-American man to totally dominate the relationship. We don't want to dominate or take total control of a relationship, but too many times, because of our strength, you become weak in our arms and you voluntarily let go of your authority and your power. When that happens, we have no other choice but to step up to the plate and take over. Because of our strength and determination, we refuse to allow our children to go without eating and we refuse to let our family fall.

We will take on two jobs to keep the bills paid. We go to work, come home and take care of the children even when you walk out on us. We pay the bills, buy your clothes and continue to build you up. We take you back after the world has chewed you up and spit you out. We nurse you back to health and put you back together again. We take you bruised and broken. We take you after you have fallen and are weak. We take you however you come; we just don't want you to stay that way! After your strength returns, we want you to continue in your growth so that you reach your full potential! And when your success returns, we want your love to remain with us!

Think back when you were growing up. Who was or is the strongest influence in your life? Your African-American mother? Your grandmother? Your aunt? Maybe you are one of the lucky ones and you had your father in your life. But, more often than not, it is the African-American mother who influences the house. Your father may have set the tone in the house, but your mother set the atmosphere. When you were hurt, to whom did you go? When you needed something, to whom did you turn? It is not because she wants to run everything, but it is because of her strength, her endurance, her influence, her determination and her strong heart.

If you have ever been locked up or in trouble, who kept in contact with you? More often than not, it is probably your African-American mother, your wife, your sister or aunt. I have seen many African-American mothers of all ages who continue to visit their incarcerated sons, no matter what they have done and no matter how old they are. I've watched as eighty year old mothers enter the prison to visit their sixty year old sons. Unfortunately, there have been too many times when mothers have to visit their husbands and their sons because the son has grown up to be just like his father! We would never consider you a waste of our time and we would never consider you as a mistake or failure. We just want you to realize that we would go to hell and back to rescue you.

In return for our dedication and sacrifice, you have turned your backs on us and have received another woman into your bed, in our places. These other women have taken your name and your fame. They have received the benefits of your strength, your power and your prosperity, simply because you think that all of us African-American women are always out to get what we can get from you and never offer anything in return! Don't you realize we have loved you until death and we just want to be loved in return?

Caucasian women are mesmerized by the beauty of your blackness. Hispanic women see you as their third choice and Asian women see you as an opportunity to leave their homeland and migrate to the land of the free, home of the brave. We, however, are here, in our own country, our own neighborhoods and in our own skin, still waiting for Mr. Right to come our way and sweep us off our feet.

Why do we care so much? It's not that we are discriminating against other races. It is because you are our first choice. You belong to us! We have labored for you and we have given birth to you. We encouraged you. We recognize your power and potential even when you don't see it yourselves. We push you to seek after your dreams.

We will protect you whenever you are accused. Whether it is in a court of law or in front of an angry mob, we will be there to defend you. We will stand by you when others want to destroy you. We picked you up when you fell and we will take you back when others toss you out! We want you to realize how much we love you because you are our brothers, our uncles, our nephews, and cousins, our sons, our fathers, the fathers of our children and our husbands. We just want to be loved by you!

Chapter 11

WE WANT YOUR LOVE

☙   ❧

*W*hat's love got to do with a relationship? Everything! Love is the foundation of every relationship. I'm not just talking about the love that a husband gives to his wife. I am also talking about the love that a son gives his mother. I am writing about and referring to the love that a husband shows to his wife and the love that a father gives to his children. There is another kind of love that should be shared between brothers and sisters. There is the love that we have for our extended family and friends. And, there is the love that we should share from heart to heart.

In our Americanized society, we use the word *love* too loosely. So loosely, in fact that, the word *love* has lost its zest, its passion and its weight. We express our *love* for things such as movies and different foods. We express that we *love* our dog or cat. We say that we *love* this movie star or that singer. The true meaning of love has been so watered down over the years that we say that we love and use the word *love* for so many trivial things. It's no wonder that when we use the word love with regard to a relationship, it's not worth the breath that it took us to utter the word and it lasts about as long as it took for the sound to register in our ears.

The word *love* has become so insignificant that many of us hesitate to say we love someone because we don't think that we will be taken seriously. We feel that the word *love*, since it has been so watered down, no longer expresses our deepest feelings and we are unable to find the words to describe what's in our hearts. When we get to the point in a relationship that we feel love for someone, we find it difficult to express our true feelings and we think our partner ought to *know* that we love them without our verbal expressions or our physical demonstrations of love.

What we have to realize, first of all, is that the word *love* is a verb and, as such, it is a word that requires action. We need to say it or express it verbally and we have to show our love in our actions, reactions and behavior. If I remember my junior high school English lessons correctly, there are three parts to a basic sentence. Those parts are the subject, the predicate or the verb, and the object. The object is the recipient in the sentence. The recipient receives the action described by the verb that is performed by the subject.

So, in the sentence, "I love you," the word "I", which is the subject, is the one performing the action. Since that word is also a personal pronoun, then the one speaking the words is identified as the actor in this sentence.

"Love" is the verb. It is the word that requires action. It is easier for us to say it than it is for us to show it. What we all have to learn to do is follow up our words of love with actions of love. To get a real understanding of the word *love* and its definition, one only has to look in the Bible, at the thirteenth chapter of First Corinthians.

There are two parts to this Biblical definition. The first part, contained in verses one through three, deals with actions that seem to portray some sense of love, but when the heart of the actor is examined, the main ingredient, which is love that fuels the action, is absent. The first part of the definitions begins like this:

> **I Corinthians 13:1 THOUGH I speak with the tongues of men and of angels, but have not love, I have become sounding brass or a clanging cymbal.**

In other words, you could have an opening line that was so smooth that it would put silk to shame. Your words and promises to your lady could be so eloquently spoken that they would fall onto and tickle her ears' fancy with the moving romance of poetic rain. You could make empty promises to your children that would make them believe you were their superman and that you were never going to leave them or forsake them. Your words could be so emotionally touching that they cause tears to fall from the eyes of the listener. This verse says you could be the world's greatest motivational speaker with such great charisma that your words would make any woman give you her most guarded treasure. But, the verse concludes, if you say all of the things that you would say to your wife, your lover, your mother, your children, your grandmother and everyone else around you, and you don't back it up with love, then all you have done is made a whole lot of noise and wasted a whole lot of breath because your words would be as empty as my stomach is after a four day fast.

> **I Corinthians 13:2** And though I have the gift of
> prophecy, and understand all mysteries and all
> knowledge, and though I have all faith, so that I
> could remove mountains, but have not love, I am
> nothing.

This verse indicates that you could be the smartest person on earth. You could be so smart that you could tell what was going to happen before it occurred, just by reading the signs of the times. You could have many degrees and have the ability to speak many languages. You could be a doctor or a lawyer or both! You could even have such faith in your relationship with God that He seems to bless everything you touch. But, the verse concludes, if you don't have love, and if you don't love, you are absolutely nothing.

> **I Corinthians 13:3** And though I bestow all my
> goods to feed the poor, and though I give my
> body to be burned,* but have not love, it profits
> me nothing.

This verse reminds us that you can feed the poor, give to every kind of charity and you can donate countless hours to different charitable organizations. You could be voted "Man of the Year" because of your many selfless sacrifices. But, if you've done all those things out of a false sense of humility and not love, you have actually wasted your time. Just because you do *good* things, it doesn't mean you are a *good* person!

At this point in the chapter, the verses take a turn and they begin to define what love does and what love does not do. To determine if you love or have love for those around you, see how you measure up to the second part of the definition:

> I Corinthians 13:4 Love suffers long and is kind; love does not envy; love does not parade itself, is not puffed up;
>
> I Corinthians 13:5 does not behave rudely, does not seek its own, is not provoked, thinks no evil;
>
> I Corinthians 13:6 does not rejoice in iniquity, but rejoices in the truth;
>
> I Corinthians 13:7 bears all things, believes all things, hopes all things, endures all things.
>
> I Corinthians 13:8 Love never fails...

Love suffers long and is kind. Love is willing to sacrifice self, for the sake of others. And, while love is putting others first, love does so without being unkind to others. Sometimes, we are willing to suffer and do without, but we constantly remind those we are sacrificing for of the things we are sacrificing. We constantly remind others that we don't have the things we want to have because we had to give to them. For the lack of a more simple way to put it, love suffers in silence!

Love does not envy or get jealous of another person's success. Love does not try to get to the top by pulling others down. Love does not applaud when others fall. Basically, love is not a *hater*, as my teenaged daughter would have explained.

Love does not behave rudely and love does not say that "you *made* me hit you"! Love treats others the way one wants to be treated. Love gives first. Love is constant. Love does not lie. Love is trustworthy and faithful.

Love would not intentionally do anything to hurt loved ones. Love continues, even when money is gone, when it seems as if everything that could go wrong does go wrong. Love is like a chain that holds relationships together. Love is the foundation upon which a marriage is built. Love will last through thick and thin. And, no matter how rough things get, love endures forever!

I Corinthians 13:13   And now abide faith, hope, love, these three; but the greatest of these is love.

The greatest gift that you, my African-American brothers, can give to us, your African-American mothers, wives, sisters, etc., is your LOVE!

I would say that most African-American mothers spend their lives giving to their sons. Sons are supposed to be strong and sons are supposed to take care of their mothers when their mothers become too old to take care of themselves.

Sons can't take care of their mothers if they are locked up in prisons. Sons can't take care of their mothers if they have been buried by their mothers because of some ridiculous gang shoot out which resulted in her son's death. If the son dies of AIDS, he can't take care of his mother. If the son takes everything that the mother has given him, and has not given her anything in return, then the mother's love is in vain.

My son is fourteen. I constantly remind him that I love him. I remind him that everything I do for him is because I love him. When I told him he could not have a BB gun that was shaped like a real pistol, he was upset with me and he thought that I was just being mean. When I explained to him that I love him, he listened when I told him that he could get arrested just for having that BB gun in his possession. I told him that because he is African-American, people would see the gun in his hand and immediately feel threatened or intimidated by him because he had the gun. I explained to him that I wasn't being mean. I wanted him to be around to take care of me when I get too old to take care of myself.

Sisters want their brothers to love them. Grandmothers and aunts want to be loved by their grandsons and nephews. Lastly, African-American women want to be loved by African-American men. This is not to say that we *need* you, or that we need a man in order to make us feel whole or complete. When God made us, He did that. Everything we need in order to reach our full potential in Christ was placed in us the moment God decided to bless us with life. We are whole women, full of strength, full of love, full of life, full of compassion, and full of passion! And, we just want to be loved by you!

As I mentioned earlier in this book, my mother and father divorced when I was three years old. Although he was never present when I was growing up, my father was always on my mind. My mother didn't talk about him because, I later learned, she didn't want to influence me with negative comments about my father. Since she didn't talk about him, I didn't ask any questions and all of the mixed feelings and emotions that I had regarding my father were my little secrets. I often wondered if he thought about me, where he was, what he was doing and whether or not he cared about me.

When I turned fourteen or so, I finally got the courage to ask questions about him. My mother immediately shared my paternal grandmother's address with me. She let me know that she had always made sure that my father's family knew where my brother and I were. Every time we moved, she let them know what our forwarding address was and she also reminded them that my maternal grandmother's phone number had not changed and would remain the same. My mother also advised me that she offered to allow my brother and me to travel to Wisconsin to visit our father's family, providing that they would pay our way there and she would pay our way back. All of my father's family members declined the offer.

My mother gave me the address and encouraged me to write a letter. At the time, my family was in Bamberg, Germany as my stepfather was stationed there. It only took me a few days to get enough courage to write. I remember that the letter was quite juvenile. I really didn't know what to say or how to say it. I remember that I introduced myself and talked about my family and my brother. I closed the letter by asking my grandmother if she knew where my father was. I also remember saying in the letter, "If you know where he is please, please tell me."

Several weeks later, I received a large envelope in the mail. It was from my grandmother. As I took the envelope from my mother's hands and ran to my room, my mind raced with the information I hoped the letter would contain. Nervously I sat on my bed and carefully opened the envelope. It was full of photos of my grandmother, my grandfather (he was deceased at the time), my uncles, aunts and cousins. There were also some older photos of my father! My excitement increased as I grabbed the letter from my grandmother and quickly scanned it for that one piece of information that would have set my heart at ease, news of my father's whereabouts.

I scanned the letter several times, before my eyes landed on the line of information that I was looking for. Unfortunately though, the line didn't exactly contain the information that I was looking for. The line read something to the effect, "I'm sorry, but I don't know where your father is..." My heart was crushed and relieved at the same time. In my mind, I quickly decided that if my father was too sorry to keep in touch with his own mother, then there was no reason he would keep in touch with me!

Although my mind was set at ease, my quest to locate my father did not end with that letter. I continued writing my grandmother. I was happy to be able to have a relationship with her. I still have some of the letters that she wrote to me. We wrote to one another regularly. I remembered that every time I ended a letter to her, I asked my grandmother if she knew where my father was and I always asked her to please tell me. I also remembered that every time, my grandmother would respond that she did not know where he was. It saddens me every time I think about the fact that my grandmother died without knowing whether or not her son was alive or dead.

After my grandmother passed away, my uncle continued to write me in her place. I kept in touch with my uncle for a while. Whenever I wrote him, I asked him the same questions regarding my father's whereabouts. He could never provide me with any information. As time passed and I matured, my father became a faint memory for me. I accepted the fact that if he really wanted me as his daughter, then I was worth looking for! Since my father was not around, I allowed my stepfather to take his place.

Let me digress for just a moment and give kudos to my stepfather. He came into our lives when I was six years old. He saw that we were living in a roach infested shack and he commented to my mother that we needed a better place to live. The shack was infested with roaches, not because we didn't keep the house clean, but because it started out as a garage, filled with junk and trash and my mother turned it into our home. We did not have foggers or other home extermination remedies back then that were powerful enough to get rid of the little pests.

Needless to say, my stepfather helped my mother secure a nicer, larger and better place for us to call home. By that time, my mother had received several pay increases on her job, so the fifty dollars a month for the rent was something she could handle. For the first time, my brother and I had a room to call our own (we shared with each other and my mother had her own room). My stepfather showed how much he cared for my mother and her two children. After their courtship, they married and we became a family. My stepfather always made sure that we had enough food and he took us out for burgers on the weekends. He constantly put his needs behind ours.

As I matured, I appreciated him more for the things that he did for me in the place of my father. He took me out to eat dinner, with just the two of us, for my sweet sixteenth birthday. He taught me how to drive a standard vehicle. He gave me his car when I started college. He walked me down the aisle when I was married. He was there when my first, second and fourth children were born. He babysat for me while I was going to graduate school and my husband was working. Even in my adult life, he has been there when I needed something. He has encouraged me in my book writing and has loaned me the money to self publish my first books. With everything my stepfather has done for me, it was easy for me to allow him to fill the void in my life that was caused by the absence of my father.

My brother, on the other hand, was not as accepting as I was. He wanted and needed the love of our father so badly that he began a vigilant search for our father that took him from one end of the United States to the other. He even tried to enter the military to find him, but was unsuccessful. Getting in touch with our father was the passion that fueled my brother's life until he ran out of gas and no longer had the emotional strength to look for him. There are too many abandoned sons and daughters who feel the same way my brother and I did.

My brother reached the point in his life where he was so devastated by the absence of our father that he decided that he would not have children, because he didn't want to run the risk of hurting them the way our father hurt him. He cried out to our mother on one occasion, saying that he wished he could just dig a hole and get a big rock that represented our father, and put the rock in it as a way to bury the entire matter—his pain and suffering, his emotional loss, his anger and frustration and his depression.

When my sister and I realized how much my brother was suffering, we went into prayer. We made our prayer agreement on a Friday. That Monday morning, I received a phone call from a contact, telling me where my father was. He was alive and well, and living in New York. This was twenty-seven years after we said our goodbyes at the train station in Fayetteville, North Carolina. Not only did my brother and I want to see our father, but so did his brothers and sisters. It didn't take long for all of us to arrange to meet my father in his home town. We were all at the train station in Milwaukee, waiting for my father's train to get in from New York. We waited in somber silence with anticipation that we were afraid to display or discuss. Finally when the train arrived and my father's small frame exited the ramp, I saw him and knew immediately that he was, without a doubt, my father. I look just like him!

Although a relationship developed between my father, my brother and me, it was strained. The question of his whereabouts and the reasons behind his failure to communicate with his family were like dark clouds lingering over and overshadowing the bond that should have been so simply defined and established. After our reunion and visit, Father stayed close to his siblings and my brother and I returned to Texas. We all kept in touch with letters and phone calls. I still have some of the letters in my possession.

Only a few short years later, I returned to Milwaukee to attend my father's funeral. During the ride from Texas to Wisconsin, I had a lingering question in my mind. I wasn't sure how I felt. I knew that I should have been sad, but since my father was virtually a stranger to me, I found it difficult to feel sorrowful. When I arrived at the mortuary to view my father's lifeless body, I walked up to him, stroked his face, and all of the emotions that I had hidden away in me came to the surface. I cried uncontrollably, as I realized that I would never have the opportunity again to get to know him better.

There are so many children in the United States who never have the opportunity to know their fathers, especially in the African-American community. I was fortunate. I was able to meet my father before he died and I still have my stepfather in my life. Although he is not my natural father, my stepfather's love for me is so great that he has become the next best thing to me for a father. He is my "dad". There are many African-American women who are rearing another man's children on her own, who would greatly appreciate someone coming into her life and filling it with love.

In my own story, it is easy to see that my brother wanted to be loved by our father. My aunts and uncles missed the love of their brother. My grandmother wanted the love from her son. I wanted to be loved as his daughter. The same holds true for so many African-Americans. We just want to be loved by you, our African-American men. You are our first choice and we want to share all that we have, all that we are and all that we hope to be, with you.

To my African-American sisters, don't just settle for anything or anybody, for the sake of love. I know that you will take being cursed out, you will take being cheated on, you will take being lied to, just to have someone to love you. Understand that you don't have to settle for less. Don't give your body away, thinking that the recipient will treasure your gift as much as you do. Too many times, he will take what he can from you and leave you with nothing but your memories of him.

Don't think that just because you are pregnant with his child that he will love you more. How many children does he already have? How many of those women did he marry? What is it about you that will make him love you more than the others? I know you want a man in your life. I know that you want to be loved. But the one thing you have to realize is that you are a queen and you deserve more. Look again at the definition of love. You will know whether or not he loves you by the way he treats you.

Everybody in the world wants to be loved. I've never met anyone who would say that they didn't want to be loved and mean it. For my African-American brother who has children with a woman that you did not marry, you can tell how much that woman loved you or how much she still loves you. Not only did she have your child, but she gave her child *your* last name, even if you were not there when the child was born. She didn't have to do that. Since she was not married to you, she could have given that child her own last name and reared the child without any influence from you and without any memory of you. With your last name, that child will know that you are his father. With your last name, that child will have a tangible piece of you. With your last name, the mother hopes that you will be reminded that the child is yours. She wanted you to be a part of her life and she wanted you to be a part of your child's life. That's how much she loves you and that's how much she wanted you to love her.

Be reminded that your child is not responsible for his or her existence. She cannot be held accountable for the irresponsibility of *responsible* adults who were engaging in behavior that required a great deal of personal responsibility! Your child is not an accident so quit treating him like one!

Chapter 12

LOVE AND HUGS

☙ ❧

*T*here was a time in our lives when my husband and I volunteered for an organization that was designed to inspire, encourage and mentor youth who were at risk. The program targeted children whose parents were in the low income bracket and children who were either already in the juvenile justice system or on their way. Although the program reached out to children of all races, as with many programs of this nature, the greatest numbers of children represented in the program were African-American. Because of the large number of African-American children in the program, my husband and I were solicited to become volunteers.

My husband and I have a heart for children and we both have experience in the Criminal Justice field. We have observed that African-Americans represent a large portion of the incarcerated offenders in the state of Texas; therefore, it was easy for us to accept the call to participate in the program. We were eager to help turn young people around in order to keep them from ending up in the adult criminal justice system.

Not long after we became a part of the program, my husband and I began to realize something about many of the youth who were incarcerated in the county's juvenile detention center. Their charges were just as diverse as they were. They ranged from simply skipping school too many times, to selling drugs, to stealing, to more violent offenses. One of the most powerful things that struck me and caused me the greatest emotional strain was the fact that some of the children were there simply because they were discarded by their parents. They were not there because of what they'd done, but they were there because of what happened to them. Here are some examples:

"Freddie" was there for murder. The reason he committed his murder was because his mother's boyfriend was beating her senseless on a regular basis. He'd already watched in fear as the boyfriend had beaten his mother on too many other occasions. As the years passed and Freddie became older, he tried desperately to help his mother whenever she was attacked by the boyfriend. He would end up getting the brunt of the beating and the mother would still end up bruised. Finally, when Freddie was old enough and when he just couldn't take any more, he obtained a gun. The next time his mother was attacked by the boyfriend, Freddie shot and killed him. Unfortunately for Freddie, his mother never filed any assault charges on her boyfriend so there was no record of the abuse. She would not come to Freddie's assistance when he was charged with the death of her boyfriend. It is a sad day when a mother wants to be loved so much that she would put the life of her son in front of a boyfriend. She failed to realize how much her son loved her.

"James" was a handsome young man. He stood over six feet tall and had the face of an Adonis. When we first met him, he was quiet and reserved. We could tell that he was from a *good* family, by the way he dressed. He always had his shirt tucked in and his belt was always on. He was always quoting scriptures and talking about the Bible. So much so, that the other kids in the detention center called him "Preach". Initially, on the surface, my husband and I could not understand why such a nice young man would end up in the juvenile justice system. Through our conversations with him, we learned that James was physically and verbally abused by his mother. He showed us a scar on his lip that was the result of him being pushed into the brick mantel of a fireplace. He was distraught by the fact that his father would never come to his rescue. So, to keep from physically retaliating against his mother, and to maintain his own sanity, James would run away.

James' mother would report him as a runaway and she would provide police with several possible locations where James would be. James would refuse to return home, and therefore, he would be placed into the detention center. He said that he tried several times to tell people that his mother was physically and verbally abusive, but he really didn't want to get his mother in trouble, so he didn't force the issue. After several run-ins with James' parents, and information we learned about James' family, we could see the validity in James' story. With encouragement from my husband and me, during James' hearing, the family court judge granted James the opportunity to live with his grandmother. It did not take long before we realized where James' mother learned how to be physically and verbally abusive. James finally received the relief he needed and wanted when he turned eighteen and joined the military.

There was "Tasha" and her sister, "Janice". They were sexually assaulted by their stepfather. They were always acting out sexually, in school. They were always skipping school, never did their homework and they always seemed to be angry. People constantly addressed their behavior but no one ever took the time to determine the reasons behind their behavior. When Tasha and Janice no longer wanted to be sex slaves, they attacked the stepfather, beating him and cutting him several times. He survived the attack and the girls ended up in the juvenile detention center for their physical attack on him. The stepfather, however, was never charged with the sexual assaults. The mother would not substantiate the girls' claim.

"Tommy" was incarcerated for being incorrigible! His only crime was being born! His mother didn't want him and neither did his father. His mother eventually left him on his maternal grandmother's door step. She was a church going women and she took Tommy to church. While he was attending church, he began taking an interest in the organ and the drums. Even though he tried to be a *good* boy, there were times when his boyish charm was overtaken by his boyish attitude. He didn't want to be the "little man" that his grandmother was trying to force him to be. He just wanted to be a boy and have fun. When he would go to the park and play ball instead of going home after school, his grandmother would say that she "couldn't handle him," and he would be taken into custody for being incorrigible. Tommy was a good kid in a bad situation. He eventually ended up being taken from his grandmother and sent to a state youth facility where he was going to stay until he turned eighteen.

"Alex" was a handsome cowboy! Yes, he is African-American and he is very good at what he does! His only crime was falling in love at a young age. As a result of his passion, he will forever have the stigma and being a young African-American male who has been labeled as a sex offender. He and his young lover took a bite of the forbidden fruit and he was left to pay the penalty and the price. The greatest problem that I have, in addition to the obvious, is that the act, being consensual, was blamed on the young man and not the girl.

To all parents, I have this to say; if we are going to hold children criminally responsible for engaging in consensual sexual activity, teach them about the horrors of sexually transmitted diseases as a part of health class, but we should NOT be teaching "safe sex" in our schools, and we should NOT be passing out condoms to students, and we definitely should NOT be ignoring the subject in our churches. What we should be doing is teaching, encouraging and instilling the principle of *abstinence* to these young people as it is the *safest* method to avoid sexually transmitted diseases, teenaged pregnancies, and juvenile incarcerations for sex related offenses!

And then there's "Cassie". She was a very intelligent, cute little eight-year-old that my husband and I met when we were volunteering with the program. She was always cheerful and she was so happy to be a part of the mentoring program. Whenever my husband and I would show up for the event that was planned, she would run up to me, throw her arms around me and say, "Mommy!" I am not the one to deny a child a hug, so whenever she, or any of the kids for that matter, would come to me for a hug, I would return one to them. I would return her hug and I wouldn't comment about the fact that she called me "mommy". She didn't say what was going on with her and I didn't ask. Cassie became attached to my husband and me. Whenever we had to take children home, Cassie would always try to get into our car so that she could be with us as long as possible. With the permission of Cassie's mother, there was a time or two where Cassie was invited to our home for the day. She enjoyed the company of my daughters and my son. For her, the day would end too quickly.

Sometime later, Cassie revealed that her brother was abused and he constantly ran away. At that time, I asked if she was abused and she said that she wasn't. When her brother stopped coming to the mentoring events, I asked Cassie where he was. She advised me that he'd run away again and this time he made it to his goal. He was trying to reach his uncle who lived in Louisiana. Cassie's brother, who was about thirteen at the time, walked and hitchhiked his way from Beaumont, Texas, to Louisiana and found his uncle. I am glad to say that the uncle fought to keep him.

Shortly thereafter, Cassie's story took on a different turn. One evening, at around 8:30 p.m., my oldest daughter came running to my bedroom, in a frantic state. She shouted, "Momma, Cassie ran away from home and she's at my friend's house!"

"What? What friend? Where?" I asked just as frantically.

"My friend called me and said that a girl named Cassie was at his house looking for her mother and she needed some help. My friend asked what her mother's name was and Cassie said, 'Mrs. Flakes'!" my daughter explained.

We went to the friend's house and picked Cassie up. She had a bicycle in her possession and she had her backpack. Talking to the friend, we learned that he was sitting at the table in his kitchen. The kitchen was next to the garage and the garage door was up. He figured that Cassie could see him sitting at the table so she entered the garage and knocked on the door. He explained that although he didn't know me, he knew that my daughter's last name is Flakes and since he had my daughter's number, he called.

We got Cassie back to our house and she explained her story. She first admitted that her mother had been abusive to her and that the abuse was getting worse with her brother being gone. She said her mother told her, "I hate you and I don't want you anymore." Cassie took her mother's words literally because they were spoken in conjunction with a beating with a switch.

The following morning, Cassie went to school as usual, only this time, she put extra clothes on her body and she put clothes in her backpack instead of her books. When school was over, instead of riding the bus home, she started walking to our house.

Understand that Cassie lived on the west side of town and at that time, we lived on the far north side. Cassie was eight or nine years old and she'd only been to our home maybe once or twice. She started walking at about three in the afternoon. When she got tired of walking, she took a bicycle from somebody's front yard and started riding the bike. By the time she reached the home of my daughter's friend, it was about 8:30 in the evening and it was very dark. Not only that, but there were highways and many busy streets between our home and Cassie's. I still can't imagine how that little girl found her way to our neighborhood. She was very close to our house as the friend only lived a few blocks away from us.

That night, I gave her something to eat and watched as she consumed every bite. After I let her rest, I told her that I had to call her mother and let her mother know that she was safe. When she vehemently objected, I had to explain further that I would be breaking the law if I kept her, knowing that she was a runaway and didn't call anybody. When I called Cassie's mother, she was not as upset as I thought she would be. She admitted to telling Cassie that she hated her and that she didn't want her anymore. She offered Cassie to me, saying, "Do you want her? I am sick of her! You can have her!"

When Cassie's mother went on to say that she was going to beat Cassie with a belt when I brought her home, I intervened. I explained that I'd fed Cassie and I lied by adding that she was asleep. "Since she's already asleep," I further offered, "why don't we just let her stay here for the night and I will take her to school in the morning." It didn't take Cassie's mother long to agree and Cassie was relived.

Since it was getting close to Christmas, I asked Cassie the same thing that many adults ask children during the Christmas season. When I asked her what she wanted for Christmas, she looked up at me and affirmatively responded, "A momma and daddy like you and Mr. Flakes." I hugged her, knowing that mine would probably be the only one that she would get.

Shortly thereafter, Cassie ended up in a youth facility because she was a runaway. My husband and I couldn't visit her because we were not her family. Cassie's mother gave up her custodial rights to Cassie and Cassie had to stay in custody until her aunt finally agreed to take custody of her. I have not seen Cassie since that time, but she is constantly on my mind.

I eventually left the program because it was so emotionally draining for me, simply because I was not in a position to return and show love to the children as I wanted to. The rules of the mentoring program clearly disallowed personal involvement with the children. It was a rule that my husband and I bent often. The children needed so much more than what the program was offering. The thing that the children needed most was the one thing that we couldn't give them as long as we were volunteers with the mentoring program. What they need most is—love.

Children have been arrested and incarcerated because they were caught stealing because they were hungry. Children have been arrested for running away from abusive homes. Children have been arrested for being misused, abused and mistreated. It has been my experience that children just want to be loved and they just need to be hugged. From the biggest to the smallest, from the toughest to the weakest, they could be red, yellow, black, brown or white, they all want someone to love them, protect them, take care of them, and cherish them. My heart constantly goes out to children who have missed out on their childhoods due to abuse and neglect. Things happen to children in this country that should never happen to them. If the fathers of these children would stand up and take their places in the lives of these children, they could make a difference.

There is a man in my church who exemplifies fatherhood and understands that children, of all ages, just want to be loved and hugged. He stands a regal six feet, six inches tall and is the tallest man in our church. At the age of 65, he is one of the elders in our church. Every Sunday, he makes his rounds throughout the church, passing out hugs to children of all ages. Children run into his open arms and eagerly receive his hug. You can even hear the voices of adults saying, "Good morning, Dad", as he grabs them in one of his genuine bear hugs. Not only does "Poppie" show love in the many hugs he gives, he also displays the enduring love that a father has for his children in the advice he shares with the men in our church. Whenever I hear him talking to some young man or boy, I think to myself that more African-American men could learn from him.

Children need love and they need to feel safe and wanted. If I had one wish, that wish would be to be in a position where I could build a safe haven for children like the ones I've mentioned in this chapter. There are several children that I would take in, this very moment, and give them a home that is full of love and hugs. I would be the mother they have always needed and my husband would be the father they have always wanted.

Chapter 13

WE WANT YOUR ATTENTION

❧ ❧

*C*ome on, my African-American brothers. Not only do we want and need your love, but we also want and need your attention. When you love someone, you spend time with them. A relationship is more than just words on a piece of paper that identifies a legal bond between two people. A relationship is like a seed that is planted. It needs attention and the proper atmosphere in order to survive and grow into something strong and healthy.

By my own observation, you spend more attention on your car than you do with your wife, your children or your mother! Look at this for a moment. You've bought rims for your car. You've bought stereos, air fresheners, added liners and many other luxury items, just to make your car look good. How much did those rims cost? When was the last time you spent that much money on your wife, just because you want her to look good? You do want your wife, the mother of your children, or girlfriend to look good, don't you? What about your children?

Let me back up for a minute. I don't want you to misunderstand what I am saying! Although I mentioned gifts, it's not always about the money! If all your family is getting from you is money and not your attention, then you are missing the point. Your wife and your children would much rather have your *presence*–they want you to be there—as opposed to your *presents*! In the matter of care, concern and attention, providing financial assistance is only a part of it. Let me continue with the car analogy so that you can see what I mean.

On your car, you changed the oil, you have gotten tune ups, fixed the flat, you became very concerned when you heard a rattling noise in the engine, and called a mechanic when you thought something was wrong with your car. These are the little things that you do to take care of your car, in order to keep bigger things from happening to it. In essence, you are looking out for your car's well being.

What about your wife? What about your girlfriend, the woman you love? There are many "little" things you could do to ensure her emotional and physical well being. You could walk up behind her and give her a hug that she didn't expect. You could kiss her without her having to ask for a kiss. You could say, "I love you," and mean it, when she least expects it. You could call her at work just to say, "Hello." You could clean up your side of the bed and pick up your clothes from the floor. You could pick your wife up from work on time and take her out to dinner. All of these things are small things that make a big difference in your marriage or relationship.

You can also thank her for washing your clothes and keeping your home clean. You can let her know how much you enjoy the food that she cooks for you. You can thank her for every time she remembered your birthday. You can show your appreciation to her by acknowledging her birthday and showering her with love on Valentine's Day. Don't wait until you are so old and broke down that no one else would want you to let your lady know how much you appreciate her. Every day you should ask yourself the question, "Have I done something for my wife today?" You can also ask the same question regarding your mother or the other African-American women in your life. And you should ask yourself the question when it comes to your children.

Think about the last time your wife or girlfriend was ill. Did you take care of her and see to her needs? The last time you were ill, who was it that took care of you? More often than not, when women get sick, they still have to take care of their responsibilities, such as cooking and cleaning, feeding the children, going to work, and taking care of everyone else's needs. Most women I have come into contact with have expressed that their men are too much like babies when they feel the slightest bit of a physical ailment! Men want to be pampered and coddled. They act as if a simple head cold is life threatening! They whine and exaggerate their symptoms and beg to be noticed. And, we women take the time out of our already busy schedules to ensure that our men have the attention that they want. All we want in return is for you to give us the same care, concern, love and attention, when we are ill.

You make sure your car's needs are being met. You pay your car note, you take care of the insurance, you get inspections and you feed it regularly by filling it with gasoline. When it's cold outside, you make sure it is safely tucked away in the garage. When it is too hot, you always park in the shade. When you are in a public place, like the park, you make sure no one gets too close because you don't want anyone to hurt your car by scratching or denting it.

You wash your car on a regular basis, stroking it gently, caressing its body, paying attention to every detail. You do all these things in order to give your car much needed, personal, hands on attention. Your wife or girlfriend wants the same attention from you! In addition to your cars, women have to compete with your friends, the ball games that you play, the ball games you watch, your hunting and fishing buddies, and all of the other interests you have in your life. All the lady in your life wants is a little bit of your attention for herself.

You have never screamed at your car, never called it names and you have never, ever struck your car with your fist or any other foreign object. The reason you don't do these things to your car is because you know that it will decrease your car's value. Face it. You pay more attention to and treat your car with more love, care and concern than you do your wife or your children!

To the ladies, let me share something with you. Sometimes men are new in the area of showing and giving love. They show their affection in ways that are not familiar to us. If that is the case, you have to take the lead and teach your man how to express his feelings. Sometimes, you have to be the example in the relationship. You have to be, to the man in your life, everything that you want and need him to be for you. If you want him to be expressive, then you have to be expressive. Don't think that your husband can read your mind and know exactly what you need or want.

Even though there are men such as the one I have described, there are also those of you who go above and beyond their responsibility when it comes to showing love and affection to your loved ones. To those African-American men who cook and clean, I applaud you! To the African-American men who provide breakfast in bed, I commend you! To the African-American men who are creative in the expression of their love, the ones who are always surprising their wives, to the ones who keep the relationship fresh, I give you a standing ovation! You deserve it!

Ladies, if your man is giving you the attention you want and need, then you should thank him and return the expressions. Too many times, we take a good man for granted! The more he gives, the more you demand! The opposite should occur. The more he gives to you, the more you should be giving to him!

My African-American brothers, before you can give us your attention and be the man we know you are capable of being, you have got to stop making excuses. We are sick and tired of the same excuses from you, my African-American brothers! When we need you to fix something, you give us your many reasons why you can't. When it comes to doing what we need you to do around the house, we get more support from our girdles than we get from you! This is not a message directed only to our husbands, but to our sons as well. We need you to cut the grass, paint the garage, fix the fence, fix the leak in the faucet, and so much more. More and more I have interviewed and conversed with many different women and I have found out that they are not alone! Not only do their men constantly make up excuses, but as time goes on and the relationship builds, the excuses increase! You may have started out making one or two excuses per week, but now you are making excuses on a daily basis and you have an excuse for everything imaginable! The crazy thing about the whole matter is, you will do for others what we are asking you to do for us, and then you will make an excuse to us and say that you can't do what we need done!

Here are some examples of your excuses. Have you ever told your lady that you were not ready for a commitment to her, but whenever she tries to break away from you and find someone else, you do everything you can to get her back? Then, as soon as she returns to you, you go right back to your same routine, making excuses that keep you from committing to the relationship! Not only is this infuriating, but it does nothing to solidify the partnership between the two of you. At this point, guys, we have to ask ourselves the question; are you worth our time?

It seems as if some African-American men, many in fact, are hesitant to make a commitment to a relationship. It is also very apparent that you want to be able to hold on to the girl you want to marry, while playing the field and maintaining your "players" card until you are ready to settle down and be committed. I would advise your lady friends that if she loves you and you're worth it, she has to be patient with you. As my grandmother has explained to me on one occasion or another, a dog will run for a long time, but eventually, he'll come back home to stay. If you want to be identified as a dog, then your lady friend will have to make the decision to wait on you and she will have to have the patience to do so. I would also advise your lady friend that if you are not worth the wait, then I pray that she will have the courage to walk away from you and not return, no matter how much you beg and plead. We African-American women have to be reminded that we were born to be queens and we deserve kings!

For those of you who are married, excuses take on a whole new meaning. Not only do you make excuses when we need things done around the house, but you also make excuses when we need your attention. When your children need you to spend some quality time with them, you make excuses. There is one thing we need to know and make clear right here and now. Your excuses are nothing but self-justified lies!

There are a few times in life when your excuses are truly legitimate. If you are incapacitated, blind, sick, cripple or a combination of the four, your excuses just might be legitimate. Even at that, if a person with no legs can compete in a foot race, then they fact that you don't have legs is really not an excuse. If a blind person can hang glide, then your blindness is no longer excusable. If a deaf person can write a symphony, then your excuses have been erased. If a quadriplegic can live alone (with a little assistance, of course), have a job, go to and graduate from college, and operate a computer, then all of your excuses regarding your physical inabilities have just been voided.

But, for the majority of you, my brothers, your excuses are made for one of three reasons: 1) you don't know how to handle the problem you are faced with and you don't want to ask your wife's assistance or opinion (because you are intimidated by her strength); 2) you don't care that your family has a problem so you tell your family that you are too busy to help and/or be available. In this instance, you may actually busy yourself with the things you want to do but can't seem to find the time to do the things your family wants or needs you to do; 3) you are just plain lazy! If that is the case, you just might be a sorry man!

For the most part, excuses are like bubbles! They are easy to make and they are mesmerizing and captivating. But in the end, they are only full of hot air and don't last beyond the moment! Excuses make us immobile. We can't move forward as long as we sit on our excuses. Excuses cause dreams to die and visions to vanish. Excuses are life's flat tire! You can't move forward into your success until you decide to change. Whenever one partner tries to move beyond the excuses of the other, the forward moving partner does so, feeling as if she (or he) is carrying dead weight! What do I say about that? Cut that dead weight off and move forward!

My brothers, you have to be especially careful when you constantly provide excuses to your family and loved ones. In your defense, your wife will repeat your excuses to her friends, your friends, your coworkers and everybody else in your world. Your children will also repeat your excuses to defend your character. And, children will take your excuses one step further and use them for themselves. This is especially true for men and their sons. Watch your son. Does his behavior look familiar to you? Do his excuses sound like something you've heard before?

Excuses are to success what a wild fire is to a forest! What does fire do to a forest? It consumes and destroys it! That is what happens to your success when you constantly make excuses regarding your ability to pursue your success. Like the wild fire that spreads in many different directions, so do your excuses. First you will make excuses in one area of your life, and then your excuse making will spread to other areas! Soon, you will find that your entire life is nothing but one big excuse! Finally, understand that as with the fire that destroys the forest and everyone and everything around it, so do your excuses. When you fail to do your part, and you make your excuses, everyone and everything around you has to pay the price.

What we all need to be reminded of is that the strength of the whole is far greater than the strength of one. When we are part of something—a family, a work group, a relationship, church body—we all have our responsibilities to perform. No one should rate himself higher than another because we all depend on each other to reach our goal. I do not recall any incident in history where a person reached his or her objective alone.

Whenever we fail to do our individual part, the body suffers! To determine who is a part of the body you are failing, take a look around you. If you are in a work situation, how many of your coworkers have to take up your slack because you don't pull your own weight? Men, take a look around your home right now and identify those things your wife has been asking you to fix. Look around at your family and see how they have to suffer as a result of lackadaisical attitude. How long must your family wait? In the family situation, when the father or husband does not do what is required of him, the wife and mother has to step up or the family suffers.

Too many times, instead of allowing the family to suffer, the mother/wife has taken on extra duties. In those instances when you are absent from the family, the mother/wife has taken on the extra duties. At that point, she is too tired to take care of other issues. So, although one part may be taken care of, there is still another part that suffers. An example would be when the woman of the house has to get a second job or work longer hours because the man of the house does not have a job and will not get a job. Sure enough, the bills may be getting paid, but the woman of the house is not at home to take care of the emotional needs of the children and when she is home, she is too tired to take care of the sexual needs of her husband.

Let me interject another message for the women who are reading this book. The solution to excuses is for the woman of the house not to accept them. We tend to take the excuses at face value and we fail to see the truth behind the lie. If you would take the time to gently ask additional questions, the excuse will eventually begin to break down and the truth will come to the surface. But, let me warn you! You may have to ask many, many questions! Additionally, the reason I say, "gently" ask questions is because in the process of your getting to the truth, you don't want to come across as being a nag!

You can also pressure your man for a specific date of completion or attention to your task. If he can't do it today, ask him when he can get to it. If he says he doesn't have the money, ask him how much it costs to get the parts and ask where you can get them so that you can help him get the job done. If he says he can't take you to dinner and a movie tonight, pull out your calendar and call out dates until he commits to one. Then, constantly (gently) remind him of the upcoming event and let him know how much you are looking forward to the time you will be spending together.

For the men, you should know that for many of the African-American women in today's times, we don't ask you for something or ask you to do something unless it is absolutely necessary! We have learned how to change our flats, we can check the oil in our cars, we know how to cut the yard, wash the car and make minor repairs around the house. We have learned how to be strong in tough times, we know how to stretch a dollar, and we are learning more and more as time goes on.

So, my African-American brothers, understand that when we ask for your help, we really need and/or want your assistance. You can make excuses if you want to and you can even blame us for your lack of ability or desire to respond to our request. Just remember these things; if you love your spouse and you want to keep her happy, know that she needs you! When you run into those situations where you genuinely can't do something, then, find somebody who can. If you are truly busy and can't do what she needs done right then and there, then give her a specific date and time when you will be able to see to her request.

In closing, there are two things I want you to remember. Firstly, as the head of your house, you set the standard and you set the tone. What is the atmosphere and condition of your house right now? Secondly, if you won't do and be what your wife/girlfriend needs you to do and be, I guarantee you she will find somebody who will!

There's just one more thing I want to add before closing this chapter. Ladies, if the man you love has a car that you would describe as a junk heap, quit complaining! Just be thankful that his car runs! If he had a "pretty" car, chances are he would begin spending more and more time with the car and less time with you!

Chapter 14

A MAN BY GOD'S DESIGN

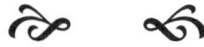

❧   ❧

I tried not to fill this book with so much Bible that the average man would not want to read it. But, as a Minister, I could not resist the opportunity to use God's Word! For those of you who feel that something is missing in your life—even if your life is full of money, women, cars and houses—you might want to read this chapter several times. The book of Psalms has this to say about you and your Creator:

> Psalm 139:13 For You formed my inward parts;
> You covered me in my mother's womb.
>
> Psalm 139:14   I will praise You, for I am
> fearfully and wonderfully made; Marvelous are
> Your works, And that my soul knows very well.
>
> Psalm 139:15   My frame was not hidden

from You, When I was made in secret, And skillfully wrought in the lowest parts of the earth.

Psalm 139:16 Your eyes saw my substance, being yet unformed. And in Your book they all were written, The days fashioned for me, When as yet there were none of them.

To my African-American brothers, I want you to know that you are God's originally designed man! He knew you before you were conceived in your mother's womb! Not only that, but He provided you with everything you would need in order to be successful. Every gift, every skill, every talent and every opportunity was created for you when He designed you.

Think about the seed principle. Practically every living thing, starts from a seed. At first glance, one might think that a seed is weak and empty. But if you consider an acorn seed, you would have to understand that it has everything in it that it needs in order to become a mighty oak tree! That one seed has within it a full grown tree! Before it is planted in the ground, it may not look like much. Even when its first branches start to bud above the ground, it looks weak. All we have to do is give the tree the right environment and it will reach its full potential.

You also started from a seed! Half of your seed came from your mother and the other half came from your father. God is consistent. If the seed of every plant contains everything in it that it needs to be successful, so do you! God designed you with His purpose for you already in His mind. To put it another way, God started with the end of your life and then filled you with the tools you would need to reach your life's goal.

According to Psalm 8 and Ephesians chapter 5, God has designed you and created you to be powerful through your relationship with Him. He made you to be valuable, beautiful, a worshipper, holy, righteous, a good worker, and faithful—to Him and to your wife. God made you to be a good father, a business man, intelligent, helpful, caring, sharing, a man of perseverance, a man of wisdom, honorable and blessed. God has created you to have dominion, which is power and authority, over all that He created. This is God's original design or plan for you!

In the Psalm 8, verse 6 reads, *"You have made him to have dominion over the works of Your hands; You have put all things under his feet"*. This word says that God has given you dominion or authority over everything He created! Let me share something with you. A man can teach a killer whale to jump up out of water, turn a flip and go back down into the water. A man can teach a bear to dance and can teach a lion to jump through hoops. A man can teach a dog to go into a lake and retrieve a duck from the water. A man can teach a killer cobra to follow the movements of a flute. Why? It is definitely not because wild animals enjoy doing stupid things outside of their nature and wild animals don't enjoy obeying man's frivolous commands. It is because the animals understand that God is the creator of the universe and they also understand that although they may not want to obey man—I've seen lions protest the jumping through hoops thing—but they must obey God! They understand that God created man to have this type of authority over the things that He has created!

Let me share something else with you about God's plan for you. Think about the seed principle again for a moment. Just as a seed has to be planted before it can reach its potential, you have been planted. You were first planted into your mother's womb. She sacrificially carried you around in her body for nine months. When you were born, you became transplanted in the lives of the people around you. You were planted in your neighborhood so that you could change it. But, instead of you changing the neighborhood, you allowed the neighborhood to change you. When you fathered your children, you were planted in their lives. You were planted in the life or lives of the women who have given birth to your children. But, when you saw the magnitude of your responsibility, you fled the scene like a scared bandit caught red handed.

Nothing that God does is accidental. Every place He planted you, He did so for a reason and a purpose. What has happened to many of you is that you have uprooted yourselves and found other places you wanted to be and you replanted yourselves there. God planted you to be the "Big Daddy" in your child's life but you decided you wanted to be the "Big Daddy" on the block. God has planted you in the life of a woman He has planned and set aside especially for you, but, instead of allowing yourself to grow and become a great influence in the place where you were planted, you uprooted yourself from your home, uprooted yourself from your neighborhood, uprooted yourself from God's plan and you started doing the things that were right in your own eyes.

What you all fail to realize is that once you were planted in your mother's womb, you started to grow. Just like with every plant that grows and bears fruit in its season, you also began to bear fruit. Understand that a tree does not consume its own fruit, but it is provided to everyone around the tree. You are that tree. You bear fruit! No matter what you have chosen to be or do, or where you are, you bear fruit! You will either bear good fruit or bad fruit, and everyone around you consumes the fruit that you bear!

Check this out, fellas. If you have a drug problem, everyone around you has a drug problem. You become their drug problem because they are consuming the fruit you are bearing. If you have a gambling problem, everyone around you has a gambling problem. When you cheat on your spouse, you are cheating on everyone around you—your children (they suffer from your lies and infidelity), your parents (they bare your shame), your friends (you make them lie for you), your coworkers (you make them cover for you) and even your pastor (he makes excuses for you). If you are an abuser, not only are you assaulting your victim, but everyone around you and around her or your children feel the pain of every blow you have inflicted upon her. The powerful thing about the fruit-bearing analogy is; you decide what type of fruit you will bear and you can change it, even in the middle of a season!

"How do I do that?" I'm glad you asked! If a farmer wanted to improve the worth or value of his fruit, he would change the condition of the soil in which the tree was planted. See? In order to change the fruit, you don't necessarily have to change the tree, all you have to do is change the ground in which the tree was planted! What a farmer would do is dig around the tree to stir up the soil and then he would add some fertilizer, some positive nutrients that will provide nourishment for the tree. The nourishment provides the tree with what it needs in order to produce *good* fruit.

You are like the tree that has been planted. The community that you live in, your environment, and the family that you were born into, have a direct affect on you. If you want to change, you may not be able to change the things around you, for they are the soil that you were planted in. But, you can, however, add something to your soil! The farmer in the illustration would add fertilizer that is eventually consumed by the tree. Your fertilizer is of a spiritual nature and comes from the Word of God! Just remember, the fertilizer has to be received and ingested by the tree. The same thing applies to the Word of God. You can't just read it and have a surface-type relationship with God and expect a change, you have to ingest the Word of God so that it becomes a part of you. When that happens, your fruit will change for the better and everyone around you will reap the benefits! If you don't know where to start, start with the words of encouragement that are printed throughout this book. It may take a while, but you will change and become new and improved!

When I was taking a graduate statistics course, we constantly talked about the statistical view of social problems. One of our topics of discussion was that of spousal abuse. Statistically speaking, spouse abusers breed spouse abusers. If you abuse your spouse, chances are your son will abuse his. There was one student in the class who had a problem with this statistic, as his father was an abuser, and he was in love with his current girlfriend. His fear was that he would be a statistic, whereby he would end up abusing his wife. The young man indicated that his older brother was already married and he was already abusing his wife. This young man said that he didn't want to become a statistic.

My response to the young man was simple. *Everyday, we wake up and decide what type of person we are going to be.* I expressed to my fellow classmate that he had already made the first step to avoid falling into his father's footsteps. He realized that his father's footsteps were not ones that were worth pursuing. I explained to him and to the rest of the class that sometimes you will have to confront and fight against your inner thoughts, because, you cannot win the battle by simply suppressing or avoiding those negative thoughts and feelings. In order to be victorious over haunting thoughts or ideas, you have to bring the thought to the forefront of your mind and attack it with positive, reinforcing thoughts that counter the negative tendency. As with the tree analogy, you will have to add some spiritual fertilizer to your life so that you will be changed from the inside out! For Christians, our only offensive weapon that we can use, in this battle of the mind, is the Word of God (Ephesians 6:10-17).

After my classmate made his confession, several others in the class indicated that they did not want to be a statistic and follow in the footsteps of their parents. I surveyed the class, asking how many of the parents of the students in the room had ever gone to college. None of my classmates raised their hands. I revealed to them that they had already broken the mold or broken the chain by choosing to do something that their parents had not—go to and finish college. I pointed out that if they have the strength, ability, courage and self-will to step outside of their parents' path in one area, there is no reason for them not to be able to do the same in whatever area they choose. Just because you are your father's child doesn't mean you have to be like him. The generational curse stops here, with you!

Now, back to God's original plan for you. Some of you will look at yourself and realize that you look nothing like the man that God designed you to be. The reason is simple. Just like with any other designer's original, we settle for cheap imitations because the original design just cost too much and we have to sacrifice and work too hard to obtain it. We all want to be identified by God as blessed among men, honorable and true. But, instead of living up to our potential, we settle for being a knock off, imperfect copy, because as much as you may want to be the man that God made you to be, you feel that His original design is just too far from you.

You feel that the original design is too perfect, too expensive and too far out of your reach. So, you settle for your bargain-hunted, basement-priced, why-pay-more-when-you-could-pay-less, garage sale, thug and mug, rapping and robbing reject, just so you can pretend to be as good as God's original design. I mean it is easier for you to lie than it is for you to tell the truth. It is easier for you to use slang and vulgarity to get your point across than it is for you to use the vast number of multi-syllable nouns, verbs, adjectives, adverbs and synonyms found in the English language. Many times, you believe that your short cuts to manhood are so much better than God's plan for you. You end up being a cheap imitation of what God really wants for you.

Look at it another way. Sometimes, we take a perfectly good original and alter it to the point where it is unrecognizable. Some of you have done just that with your lives! You have taken God's plan for you and altered it to fit your own lustful desires. Where God has created you to be a leader of young men, you have taken your God- given authority and used it to solicit our boys into your web of criminal activity and/or homosexual behavior. Where God has made you a psalmist to sing praises to Him, you want to make a quick dollar, so you sing songs about sex, drugs, lies, killing and stealing. No matter how far you have strayed from His plan, deep down inside of you is still the man that God wants you to be, but you have altered His design!

Not only am I a writer, but I am also a designer. I like to design clothes for myself and for my children. Whenever I design something, I see the finished product in my mind, before I do anything else. I see how the article of clothing is going to look. I see the color and the type of fabric I want to use. I see what patterns and prints I may want to include in the outfit. I can even see the zipper, buttons and other notions I may need for the outfit. I see all of these things before I begin to make my plan on a piece of paper.

Look at the sixteenth verse of Psalm 139. It reads, " *Your eyes saw my substance, being yet unformed. And in Your book they were written, the days fashioned for me, when as yet there were none of them.*" God saw you in His mind before you became the results of your father's famous five minutes of passion! He knew what you looked like, how you were going to walk, what your voice would sound like, what color your eyes and your hair were going to be and He even knew your name! He knew how He was going to use you for His glory and He made sure that He provided you with everything you needed to meet His demand.

Here is another analogy. Say, for example, I design a car for my son, since men and boys really like cars. The car that I design for him is the one that he has always wanted and it is the one that is perfect for him. The car is something that will benefit him and give me glory at the same time because it is my own design, with my name on it. I design the car and give him everything he needs to make the car. I give him the parts, the screws, the bolts, the paint, the leather for the interior, the pipes, the tires, the rims, the wrenches and screwdrivers, and even some extras like a 6-CD changer, stereo and speakers. I give my son everything imaginable to make this car especially for him. His car is unique and there is not another one like his.

Not only do I give him everything he needs, I also give him specific directions and instructions to build the car and a manual to operate the car after he builds it. Then, I tell him if he needs any help, all he has to do is call me. There is absolutely no reason why my son shouldn't be able to successfully build his car.

After I give my son all that he needs, there are several things that could happen. First, my son could try to build the car without referring to the instructions that I gave him. Many of you have tried to put some simple things together without reading the instructions and, if you would admit it, you had problems! Sometimes, your finished product looked nothing like the picture on the box! A car is too complicated to build without instructions. Your life is too complicated to live without the assistance of some instructions! God has given us all of the wisdom and knowledge we need, in His Word. We have all of the information we need in order to live the way He has commanded for us to live. My African-American brothers, you don't need a shade tree mechanic to help you live to your fullest potential, as God has provided you with His Holy Spirit to guide you.

The second thing my son could do is choose not to make the car at all! If he makes that decision, he will live far beneath his potential and he will go without. He would live his life wondering what could have happened if he had surrendered to my instructions, persevered and followed through. After reading this book, there will still be some of you who will live the rest of your lives wondering what God has in store for you. As long as you do nothing to improve your life through your relationship with Christ, you will continue to go without, wondering what could have happened if you had surrendered to God's instructions and His will for you. You would go on wondering what gifts and talents He provided you with in order for you to obtain your success.

Thirdly, my son could start out making the car, get bored, say that it is too hard, and stop. We sometimes start out doing all of the right things. There are many of you who started out going to college, you were married, you wanted to make your wife happy and you wanted to take care of your children. There are also many of you who started out in church. But, somewhere in your life, you either got bored or things seemed hard, so instead of working harder to make it through, you took the easy way out and quit. We sometimes start out excited about becoming the person that God has designed us to be, and before too long, we get bored with being holy, faithful and honorable, and we stop. We think to ourselves that being holy is too hard and too complicated, so we put the partially built car in the garage and go back to our old ways.

Another thing that could happen is that my son could start out making the car, but in the process, he could get hurt. Let's say that he gets hit in the head while he is installing something underneath the car. He could decide, at that point, to stop working on the car because in his mind, every time he attempts it, he gets hurt. Some of you, my African-American brothers, are the same way! You start out trying to do better and you lose friends, so you stop. You try getting a job and get turned down, so you quit trying and go back to your hustle. You start going to church and paying your tithes, your water gets turned off and your wife starts complaining, so you stop.

God has never promised that you would not get hurt and He never promised that this journey would be easy! As a matter of fact, the Word is full of scriptures that warn us to the contrary. He instructs us to remain joyful when we have problems and when we are tempted. He reminds us that He will be with us through whatever we go through. The problems that we have are designed to put us in a position where we trust God even more.

Maybe my son would start out making the car, but then he comes to the conclusion that the car was not exactly what he thought it should be. So, he begins altering the plan, adding mag wheels and fiber glass pipes, making the bass louder, adding hydraulics, taking out the back seat and replacing it with more speakers. He could also change the color of the paint and alter the muffler. By the time he gets finished, the car looks nothing like the one that I designed!

This is how many of you, my African-American brothers, have treated your lives. When God's idea of manhood is in direct contrast with what your vision is, you begin altering God's plan and vision for you. He has predestined you for great things, but when you don't go by His rules and His plan, you end up with less than what He has to offer. In essence, God has given you the plans for a Cadillac and you have presented Him with a wreck and a mess!

Let me remind you that in the beginning, when I started writing this analogy, I let my son know that if he has a problem with anything that I have given him, all he has to do is call me for instructions! If you are having problems with the plans that God has for you, if you don't understand them, or if you have lost your plan, all you have to do is call Him by seeking Him in prayer! He's still there, waiting to hear from you.

I know that sometimes we feel that we have gotten so far off track that we will never be able to get back where we are supposed to be. Let me share this with you. It is important for you to know and realize that no matter what you have done in your life or what you have gone through or what has happened to you, you are still God's man and He still loves you. He still wants what's best for you. Everything He has promised to you is still available to you. No matter where you are in your life, God still has more for you! You have never decreased in your importance or your value to God.

Take a one hundred dollar bill, for example. If I stood before you in a group of young men and asked, "Who wants this one hundred dollar bill?" How many of you would raise your hand? My guess is that all of you would raise your hands. If I asked, "Why would you want it?" I imagine all of you would say that you would want the one hundred dollar bill because it is worth one hundred dollars. That is simple enough.

What if I tore the bill in half and asked if you would still want it? Again, your response would be that you would still want the bill because you can tape it back together, it has not lost its value and it is still worth one hundred dollars. Even if I balled the bill up, tossed it on the floor and stepped on it, you would still want it. You would reason that you can pick the bill up, dust it off and straighten it up. And, regardless of its condition, the bill is still worth one hundred dollars.

Furthermore, if I took the bill and dumped it into a bucket of mud, and asked if you still wanted it, you would probably indicate that you did. Again, you could take the bill out of the mud, wash it up and clean it up and it is still worth one hundred dollars. If I took the one hundred dollar bill, wrapped it around a rock, tied a string around it and tossed it into a pool, you would still want it even if you had to dive into the pool after it, or drain the pool because you can't swim. Lastly, if the bill has been locked away in a box for 25 years, you would still want it, because it still has value. No matter how long it was locked up, it never lost its value.

Check this out. It is the enemy's job to treat you the same way. Satan will present you before God and ask God if He still wants you. God would respond that He still wants you, because He created you to have worth and value, and no matter what has happened to you, you are still valuable to God. If you were ripped into pieces by Satan, God still wants you because He knows he can put you back together again. If you feel as if you have been dropped to the ground and stepped on, God still wants you because He can and will pick you up, and straighten you out! You are still worth something to God! Even if the devil has taken you and placed you into a muddy pit, God will come to your rescue! He knows He can dig you out of your pit. He can wash you off and clean you up!

If you have been locked away for many years because of a crime you committed, you must realize that you have never lost your value! If the devil has tried to destroy you with drowning suicidal thoughts, God will reach down into the suffocating depths of your depression and rescue you. You are worth it because you have never lost your value! God has taken the time to create you and make you unique. You are that important to Him, no matter where you are or what you have done. If you just call out to Him, He will come to where you are and deliver you!

Chapter 15

KINGS VS. PAWNS

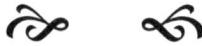

❧   ❧

*M*y daughter shared a dream that she had with me. In the dream, she was sitting at a small table where a chess board was set up. In front of her were a bunch of pawns and a queen piece. A voice spoke and said, "You're a queen. And, you want a king, right?" A king piece appeared and the pawns disappeared, one by one. Then the voice asked, "Why are you still holding on to pawns?"

She asked me for the interpretation of the dream, even though she already had her suspicions. At the time, my daughter had been going through relationships like women go through pantyhose. We put them on in the morning and before the day is over, something happens to ruin them. We toss the pantyhose out and go to the store for another pair. Because we know they will run, no matter how expensive they are, we get the cheapest brand   of pantyhose going, and we wear them for as long as we can. My daughter was jumping in and out of relationships just that quickly. Not because she was *fast* or *loose*, but because the relationships were *cheap* to begin with and she knew and felt in her heart that they were not going to last.

I explained my daughter's dream to her. The dream revealed how she felt about herself. She did not feel as if she deserved to be a queen. As such, she did not feel she deserved to be loved by someone that she felt was better than she is. My daughter felt that the more she liked an African-American brother and the better she treated him, the more he took advantage of her. She felt as if something was wrong with her. We talked, like the woman at the beginning of this book, and I let her know that there is absolutely nothing wrong with her. I also shared that the dream was to let her know that God made her to be a queen. The dream also meant that all of the men she'd been dating were like pawns. In life, I explained, pawns keep you from your king. The Lord wanted to bless her with the king He created to love her, but as long as she was messing with pawns, she was blocking the way to her king.

After I explained the dream to her, she asked me how to tell if the man she was with was a king versus a pawn. I was so happy to explain to her that just like on a chess board, there are many pawns, but only one king. Pawns take up space. They are expendable. They don't make points and they are ineffective as leaders. Pawns are those of you who are takers and not givers. My brothers, if you are only in a relationship for what you can get from your partner, you are a pawn. If you don't want to be responsible and don't want responsibility, then you are a pawn. Pawns are always overtaken in the game of chess and in real life. Pawns, in life, come in all shapes, sizes and colors. Just like on the game board in chess where there are black and white pawns, on the game board of life, pawns are black, white and every color in between. As long as a man has a pawn's mentality, he will never, ever be a king!

Additionally, to the brothers, it is important for you to know that you are to be a king over your household, the king over your family, pretty much like a king of over his kingdom. The king takes care of the people he rules. He does not abuse his citizens or else they will rise up against him and dethrone him. The king makes sure that his citizens have food to eat, shelter, and protection when the enemy comes. Not only that, but when the king is on the throne and ruling as he should, the kingdom is at peace and at rest. When the king is absent from the throne, either the queen will rise up and take his place or the kingdom will end up in chaos. Men, how many of you can truthfully judge your house hold? Is the queen in charge because you, the king, are absent? Or is the kingdom—the household—in chaos because of your absence? The only way for families and households to be at rest is for the kings to take their places and take hold of their responsibilities.

Lastly, my sisters, if you are living with a pawn, you don't have to toss him out! Start praying for him and start praying for yourself. Just because he is a pawn today, doesn't mean he has to remain a pawn! God can take him, reshape him and remold him into the king that God designed him to be! In the same manner that my son takes his building blocks and makes a house, then he takes the same building blocks and makes a car or motorcycle, God can take the same stuff that your husband, father, brother, or son is made out of and change him! God is the great re-builder! He can take your raggedy pawn and remake him into a righteous king!

THE MAN WHO WOULD BE KING

To my African-American brother, I know you may be asking yourself about your own position. You may be reviewing where you are right now in your life, trying to determine if you are a king or a pawn. The best way for you to determine where you are is to look at where you want to be. I know without a doubt that you all want to be kings and not pawns. Even though there will be times when you will be in a position of followship, you still know that there will be times when you will be called upon to be a leader and in essence, a king.

The first order of business in determining if you are a king or a pawn is for you to understand what a leader is and what a leader does. You have to understand the aspects and characteristics of leadership. In order to be a leader, we have to understand that leadership does not mean dictatorship. A person can be a dictator whereby people respond not out of a desire to do well or out of love for the leader, but they respond out of fear of retaliation. In a dictatorship, there is no love, there is no desire to change, and there is no desire to please the one in charge.

Leadership is not synonymous to power or authority. One can be in a position of power and not be an effective leader. You could be in a position of authority and still not be an effective leader. What good does it do you to be a supervisor that nobody respects? I have worked for several people who fit that description. These people were in great positions of authority and power, but they were very poor leaders. The world has many people in positions of power and authority, but the world does not have enough leaders.

Leadership is the ability to influence and encourage others to act. It is the ability to promote positive change in others. For the most part, a leader, or a *good* leader, encourages those under his or her leadership to act positively or perform positive actions.

Leadership should always be directed towards those we are leading. What is best for the people? How can I help the people? How does this decision, this program, this policy, or this law affect the people? When one's vision turns inward, it is no longer a leadership role that one is operating in, but one of dictatorship fueled by greed. There are many companies and corporations that have suffered greatly and have subsequently failed due to the philosophy and vision of the leader or leaders turning inward and becoming more directed towards the fulfillment of one's own desires.

There is a very dirty four letter word in the English language. It is a word that has caused many wars and has fueled the minds of many criminals. This word has destroyed families and has caused many businesses to fail. This word is so powerful, that the only one who can control it, is the person who has possession of it. I have used this four letter word through out this book. The word is "S-E-L-F"!

When this word is combined with other words, the conjunction could result in great and positive things, or it can result in devastatingly negative things! Some of the conjunctions include: self- motivated, self-indulgent, self-pride, self-esteem, and self-destruction. These particular combinations of words could have destructive impact, depending upon the heart of the person who speaks and lives these words.

On the other side of that coin, there are words, that have their success or failure based on the same word; self. Words like perseverance, success, persistence, motivation, determination, and discipline have great and positive results when *self* gets involved. When you, my African-American brothers, become self-motivated and self-disciplined to pursue your goals, you won't need anyone to constantly and consistently poke and prod you and pat you on the back in order to get you to in a position where you will be successful.

Secondly, in order to identify whether or not you are a king or a pawn, you need to look at some examples. One thing that I have learned in my life is that if there is something that I want to do or be, I need to examine the examples that are already in place and pattern myself after the successful models, while interjecting my own creativity and expression. To see if you are a leader, let's look at some leaders and see how you measure up. Briefly, I want to talk to you about three different leaders. These three leaders were all kings. The first one, took his throne, the second one was given the throne, and the third on was born to reign on the throne.

SAUL
(I Samuel 9 through II Samuel 21)

The first king of Israel was chosen by the people of the nation. Fueled with their own greed and desires, the people chose Saul as their king because he *looked* like a king and he *looked* like a leader (I Samuel 9:2). Saul was taller than most and he was physically strong. He was the physical epitome of power, authority and success. The people wanted everything that Saul's strong physique represented. Therefore, he was appointed as the leader of the nation and the people had their king.

Unfortunately, Saul did not have the heart or the mind of a leader. He did not possess the wisdom, skills, and knowledge that are pertinent to leadership. He did not have a vision for the people. Therefore, the people got more than they bargained for when they selected Saul as their king.

Saul ruled the people with his own agenda in mind. He selfishly taxed the people; he ruled with a hard hand, he wanted things done his way. Instead of a leader, the people received a dictator. The throne was designed as a seat of representation for the people and Saul took the power of the throne and used it for himself.

Too many people try to obtain leadership roles by "looking" like a leader. They try to hold their heads higher than those around them. They try to look professional at all times. They try to equate leadership with something on the physical level. There are people in leadership positions because they took the throne, so to speak, by lying, cheating, backbiting, clawing, scratching and forcing their way to the top. Many of these people find that they are lonely in their success because they have destroyed the spirits of those around them in their climb to the top.

To my successful African-American brothers; you look good in your double breast suits and your alligator shoes. You have excelled in the business world and you have made your mark. Please remember that leadership is founded in the condition of your heart. What's in your heart? Do you want to rule or do you want to be a leader? How many people have you led to the top of the mountain with you? Look behind you. Is anyone following in your footsteps or is your road to success covered with the bodies of those you destroyed on your way to the top? Instead of taking, a king or leader gives back.

DAVID
(I Samuel 16 through I Kings 2)

The next king that I want to mention is David (I Samuel Ch. 16).

He was anointed and appointed to be the king over Israel at an early age. He was chosen by God because his heart was in the right place. As a result of his faithfulness to God, the throne was given to him. Early on, he exhibited the characteristics of a leader. He had the ability to influence a change in the group of men who followed him. These people were broke, disgusted with Saul's dictatorship, their pride was bruised and they felt like failures. Before David became king, he influenced these men to the point where they were transformed from their weaknesses and failures to where they became mighty men of valor.

Although David had the heart of a king and the heart of a leader, he did not have the mind of a leader. His thoughts became plagued with his own lustful desires and the object of his desires was another man's wife (II Samuel Ch. 11). He used his position as the leader to seduce the woman into his bed. Then he used his influence to have the husband of the woman carry his own death warrant to the commander at the front line of a battle. The commander, in his love and respect for the king and leader, obeyed David and had this man put on the front line where his death was eminent. David disregarded what was in his heart and sought after the desires of his mind and flesh.

My African-American brothers, when you operate in your position of leadership, be it husband, father, or CEO, don't forget what is in your heart—that should be, the good of the people! David started out well. He operated in the leadership role before he became king because leadership, which is compassion for the people, was in his heart. But, when the voice in his mind and the call of his flesh overshadowed the still small voice in his heart, he failed in his role as the leader.

Know that, just like David before he was actually crowned king, you don't have to have a title, or a position of power or authority, to be an effective leader. You can influence the young men around you by your positive presence. You don't have to be the strongest or the smartest. All you have to do is have enough compassion to put other people first. You can be a leader wherever you are, just by exhibiting leadership qualities and characteristics. The important thing for kings to remember, even when positions of leadership are inherited, you must maintain the heart and mind of a leader at all times. Don't take the gift of your leadership position for granted.

The Bible gives us an example of such a challenge and such a man in the life of Joseph, one of the twelve sons of Jacob (Genesis Ch. 37). Although Joseph had ten older brothers, he was the one who became the leader for his family. He was kidnapped and sold into slavery. But, even as a slave, he showed great leadership skills. He even influenced a positive change in the man who had ownership of him. So much so that when Joseph was falsely accused of rape, by Potiphar's wife, instead of having Joseph put to death, Potiphar had Joseph put in prison. While Joseph was in prison, he continued to operate in a position of leadership. He influenced the other prisoners and he influenced the jailers. He was such an influence and such a leader that news of his abilities won him the pharaoh's favor (Genesis Ch. 39 and 40).

In one day, Joseph went from serving a life sentence for a crime he didn't commit to being the second in command in the land of Egypt (Genesis Ch. 41)! Joseph was rewarded a great position of power and authority. The only one in Egypt who had more authority than Joseph was the pharaoh himself. Understand that Joseph did not wait until he was given a position in order to perform the duties and responsibilities of a leader.

He did not wait to be given power before he operated in the position of leadership. You, my African-American brothers, can be a leader right where you are. As a matter of fact, put yourself to the test. Right where you are, begin operating as a leader, influencing and encouraging positive change in the people around you.

JESUS OF NAZARETH
(The Gospels of Matthew, Mark, Luke and John)

The third king I want to talk to you about is the One who was born to be King. He is none other than Jesus of Nazareth. He has been called the Christ, which means Anointed One or Empowered One. He has been hailed as the King of kings and the Lord of lords.

One thing that we cannot ignore is the facts concerning Jesus of Nazareth. Whether we believe Him to be the Son of God or not, the facts still remain. There is a record of His birth. I believe that it was in God's plan for Him to be born during tax season, just to ensure that there was a record of His birth. There are records, Biblical and non-Biblical, that reference His life. And, there are records of His crucifixion and death.

Whether you believe Him to be the Son of God or not, one cannot ignore the fact that He was and still is the most phenomenal, most powerful, most charismatic, leader of all time! During His life, He captivated His audiences with His presence. All He had to do was show up! Thousands of people would come just to hear what He had to say and when He spoke, everybody listened! He spoke to people on their level. When He was talking to shepherds, He used sheep talk. When He was talking to soldiers, He used war stories. When He was talking to prostitutes He told them what real love was. When He spoke with the educated Pharisees and Sadducees,

He used the Torah and the Law, because they were so fluent in its contents (Mark 7:3-13).

Even now, more than two thousand years after His death, burial and resurrection, and after only three and one-half years of motivational speaking tours and active training seminars, He is still training leaders, He is still influencing people to engage in positive behavior, people still imitate Him, people still learn from Him and people still want to be like Him. There are more books written about Him, in more languages, than any other man in history. He is still the most talked about person in the world. He is still changing lives and making a difference in the lives of people of all ages, races, nationalities, educational levels and socioeconomic backgrounds.

Jesus the Christ was so phenomenal that with His life, He split time! Think about it for a moment. Calendar years are divided by His life! We often see history dated with the abbreviations "A.D." and "B.C." The time before His birth is known and referred to as "B.C.", which quickly translates to Before Christ. And the latter years, the years after His birth are referred to as, "The Year of Our Lord" (that's what A.D. means—not "after death")! The "A.D." stands for two Latin words, "Anno Domini", which means "in the *year* of the *Lord"* (Thorndike, E.L., and Clarence Barnhart [1992]. Student Dictionary. New York: Scott, Foresman and Company). So, every time we say the year 2006, we are actually saying the 2006th year of our Lord and Savior Jesus Christ! This means that our Lord and Savior has been on the throne and has been reigning for 2006 years! He's not dead as the words "after death" would imply! He is alive and well and still ruling and reigning! That's good news! (I just had to throw that in there, it was too good to keep to myself!)

Now, back to the leaders. What separates a king from a pawn? Adolph Hitler was a pawn that infected the world. His leadership was more of a dictatorship, and his goals and agendas were all to satisfy his own lust. Although he infected the world with his poison, he didn't have enough impact to change the world. Hitler just resulted in being a disease that needed to be cured. Unfortunately, there are still people carrying around his infectious virus, even today.

There were other pawns also such as Napoleon Bonaparte, Alexander the Great, and Caesar Augustus. These leaders had great armies at their beck and call. There were temples built in their honor, but despite their greatness, their fame and leadership ended when they died. How did Jesus Christ do it? How did He become the greatest leader, King and ruler of all time? Firstly, He trained others to be leaders. He started out with twelve men that He chose to personally train to be leaders. He trained them to take His place as a leader, after Him. He spent time with them, providing them with guidance, wisdom, skills and knowledge. He led them by His own example. He corrected them with gentle rebuke and encouraged them with love and compassion. He was not afraid that they would be better than Him or that they would do more than He did. In fact, He explained to the twelve men that it was His goal to put them in position where they would succeed Him and do greater works than He did (John 14:2).

Fellas, what you have to remember is: you will not always be here! Sooner or later, someone is going to take your place. The only way to ensure that the quality of your leadership will continue, after you move on, is to train those around you to take your place! If you are going to be effective leaders, you must train your sons and daughters to do greater things than you did and teach them to achieve more than you did. Don't be fearful of their success, especially if you are the one who groomed them to reach their goals!

Secondly, Jesus the Christ kept His focus on the people He was leading. He did things that were in the best interest of His followers. He sacrificed His own desires and goals so that the people around Him would reap the benefits of His life. He laid His authority aside and He put His power aside and allowed Himself to be influenced by the needs of the people. Thirdly, Jesus was not afraid to stand up for what is right. When a woman was falsely accused of adultery, there were people who wanted to stone her to death (John 8:1-11). Christ responded by telling the woman's accusers to identify the one among them who had not done anything wrong in the course of his life. And, let the guiltless one be the first to throw a stone. None of the woman's accusers could do so.

Jesus let His followers know that His ministry was not about being king, it was not about being the richest person, nor was it about being the strongest or the most powerful. Jesus let them know that His purpose was not even about being the most popular! Nor was it about gaining wealth or having a seat of honor before other men and kings. He let them know that being the leader, king, or the greatest, was and is always about the people we serve. Being the greatest king was not about the number of shoulders you had to stand on to get where you are, but it is about the number of people who can stand on your shoulders and reach their goal because of your sacrifice. If you can serve and be a servant to the people, in love and with compassion, then you have the ability to be a great and effective leader.

The one who would be a leader or king is not the one with the biggest gun, but it is the one who makes the biggest impact. The leader is not the one who destroys life, but he is the one who changes lives. The leader believes love is a sign of strength and not weakness. The one who would be a leader is not the one who beats you down, but the one who builds you up. The one who would be a leader is not one who breaks the rules, but he sets the standards.

My African-American brothers, you were born to be leaders and kings. If you want to grow into leadership and if you want to know what you need to do in order to succeed as a leader, you must pattern yourself after the greatest leader of all time. You must be kind, gentle, a trainer, a giver, and have compassion for the people under your leadership. You must be willing to make a sacrifice when it comes to your own feelings, your own desires, your own wants and lusts. You must stand up for what is right, even when it goes against the majority. You must be a person of integrity, trustworthy, a person of your word. If you want to be a great leader, you must possess the wisdom and knowledge to lead your followers in the direction that is for their good. You must not be afraid to provide your followers with the skills, wisdom, knowledge, and courage to succeed you and take your place.

When you have succeeded in these things, then you are a leader in the true sense of the word. You will be a true leader when people refer to you as the one who inspired them and encouraged them to be all that they can accomplish. When you have succeeded as a leader then, perhaps, the next time someone is called upon to speak on the topic of leadership, you will be the one identified by the speaker as the greatest, most phenomenal leader of all time.

Men have to realize that they are in a very powerful position. Men and fathers can change the world! You can change the world by the way you teach and train your children! If you teach them not to hate, they won't hate! If you teach them not to be prejudice, then they won't be. If you teach them to give, love, be fair, be honest and strong, then they will grow up with those characteristics. Your children and the children you influence are a picture of you! When you look at them, what kind of a reflection do you see?

You were born for a purpose and the devil is doing whatever he can to keep you from reaching your full potential. If you want to live to your potential and need some encouragement, email us at: bfap@ragenterprise.com.

Chapter 16

A PRAYER FOR AFRICAN-AMERICAN MOTHERS

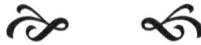

⊷   ⊶

*T*he one fact that none of you can deny, my African-American brothers, is that you have your beginning, your origin or your roots in an African-American mother. Even if your father is African-American and your mother is not, you would still be able to find your African-American mother in your paternal grandmother. If you are multiracial and you identify yourself as African-American, you may have to go back several generations, but you will still find your African-American mother somewhere in your history. I guarantee you that she will be there somewhere along the pages of your past ancestors. This book was written for you, my brothers, but this prayer is for your mothers.

For all of the African-American women who have ever given birth to a son, I pray for you. If you have reared another woman's African-American son, I pray for you even more. I pray that God will give you the strength to rear your son to be a king. Even if you have to fight against his strong will, even if you have to pull against his determination to do what's right in his own eyes, and even if you have to war against his stubbornness and his attitude, I pray that you will outlast his rebellious nature. I know that God has given you the insight to see beyond his wild imaginations and his desires for a quick rise to fame and fortune. I pray that He will enable you to cut through your son's confusion and misdirection in order to keep him on the right track.

For all of the African-American women who have had to work, fight and struggle just to keep your children together, food on the table and clothes on their backs, I pray that God will bless you with sons and daughters who will appreciate your sacrifice. I pray that He will help you to rear your children in the absence of their fathers. I pray that He will encourage you daily, with the breath of His presence. I know that He hears you when you cry yourself to sleep at night and I know He sees the tears that fall from your eyes when no one else is looking. I pray that God will bless you with peace and that He will give you joy, for joy is misery's antidote.

I know that you will give your life for the sake of your son. If he was in a situation that was about to take his life, you would step in and do all that you could do in order to rescue him. I pray that God will bless you for your sacrifice, for the love you exemplify for your son is the love that God expresses for us in His Word. You, my African-American mother, are an example of the sacrificial, never ending, unconditional love that God has for us. I pray with all of my heart, that when your life is over, your sacrifice will not be in vain.

For every African-American mother who has turned her own son in because of his criminal behavior, I commend you! I pray that God will turn your guilt in to praise. I pray that He will help you to understand that you were not "snitching" on him, but you stood up for what is right and when he would not be obedient to everything you have taught him, you turned him in to keep from destroying others. You were not sacrificing him, but you were letting him go so that he would be in a position to come to himself and return to God, for he is your prodigal son. I rejoice with you because you have shown that you are willing to put aside your own pain, in order to do what your son would not do for himself. I know that even though he may not be willing to forgive you immediately, he will eventually because you will still be there when all of his friends are gone.

For those of you, my brothers, who have never experienced your mother's love, I pray for the women who gave birth to you. I pray for the mother who died while giving birth to you, because from the moment you were born, she sacrificed her life for you. I pray for the mother who left you on someone else's doorstep. I pray for the mother who allowed her drug addiction, her alcoholism and her vice-filled way of life to get in the way of being the mother to you that she was intended to be. I pray that God will forgive her for abandoning you and I pray that you will forgive her for leaving you, for that was her greatest mistake. You have missed out on one of God's greatest gifts, the love of an African-American mother. I pray that God will help you to forgive your African-American mother for the mistakes she's made in her moments of weakness.

For every son who was left to cherish the memory of his African-American mother, I pray that God will ease your pain as He gently reminds you of your mother's love for you. For those of you whose mother is still living, I pray that God will remind you that she is the reason you are here. I pray that God will remind you that she gave birth to you and you owe your life to her. I pray that God will remind you to return to her the love that she has so unsparingly given to you.

Chapter 18

WORDS TO LIVE BY

❧   ❧

*O*n a regular basis, I speak to the offenders during the orientation process on the facility where I am currently employed. During my presentation, I offer them words to live by. These short pieces of verbal instructions are designed to provide them with meaningful bits of encouragement that will help them to stay focused and keep their eyes on the greater prize. I just want to share some of those words with you.

I could complain, but I won't! Whenever things go wrong and sometimes when things are going good, there is still something in your situation that you could complain about. You could have a good job where your hours are great, the people you work with are easy going and you have a boss worth working for. But, you still have a problem with the paycheck you receive for the services you have rendered. When you have more month than you have paycheck, you have reason to complain. When you have sweated all day at work and you go home to more work, you could complain. In all that you do, all that you need to do and don't have time to do, you could complain. You have the power to decide whether or not you will complain about your situation. Remember, even though you are justified, you could complain, but decide against it.

Hold on to the reigns of your responsibility or else you will end up with a runaway carriage. Think about everything you are responsible for—your household, your job, your children and your parents. You are responsible for the bills that need to be paid. You have a car note to pay and so many other responsibilities. Imagine that you are a handler on a stagecoach and everything that you are responsible for as being inside the stagecoach. In life, the road gets rough and the ride gets bumpy. Sometimes the ride can be down right dangerous. The only way for you to manage the stagecoach is to hold on to the reigns. You have to handle your responsibilities in the same fashion or else you will lose control and the results could be devastating.

Turn the stumbling blocks of your past into stepping stones for your future. First of all, realize that you can't trip over a mountain. You can see a mountain and you do whatever you need to do in order to go around it or avoid it altogether. The things in life that trip us up are the little things. For example, you won't ingest a kilo of cocaine at one time. You know that it would kill you. You get hooked on drugs a little at a time, over the course of time. Drug addiction creeps up on you.

As I have said before, we all make mistakes. The difference between successful and unsuccessful people is the way they handle their mistakes. The first step to correcting a mistake is admitting you have one. Before many of us go to a doctor's office, we have to admit that something is wrong with us and we need assistance in getting better. The same thing is true for addiction. If you are not willing to admit to a drug or alcohol problem, then your family can't help you, neither will all of the counseling in the world help you. Again, the little things, such as self admission, will either trip us up or set us up on the road to our success. Once you admit your problem, your admission becomes the first step towards a better future.

Don't just settle for the light at the end of the tunnel! Hold out and press towards the pot of gold at the end of the rainbow. Remember me telling you that when I decide to write a book, I don't just meditate on the first page? If I did just think about the first page, how much of a book do you think I would get written or typed? The first page! What do you think my friends and family would say if I brought that first page to them and said, "Look at my book! I'm writing a book!" The first thing that my friends and family would say is, "Okay, where's the rest of it?"

They realize that the first page is only the beginning. It is so easy to begin something, but it takes perseverance, persistence, consistency, dedication and determination to finish something. Making a choice today to change your life for the better is only the beginning. Even after you have made positive steps for, let's say, six months, that's still only the beginning. The beginning of your road to success is only the light at the end of the tunnel. The pot of gold at the end of the rainbow is the rest of your life! Imagine, if you will, that everyday you have left to live is one of those gold coins. Everyday you have to ask yourself, what did I do with my gold coin today. Did you live a day that was worthy of the gold coin's value or did you take your gold coin and flush it down your crack pipe and then wash it down with a forty ounce? Perhaps you just sat on your gold coin all day long and when the day ended, you couldn't find it. It's your pot, it's your gold, it's your life! What are you going to do with it?

Forgiveness is to a relationship what penicillin is to disease. My African-American brothers, there are many of you who have injured and/or destroyed relationships with those who are closest to you. You have children that you have neglected, there are the mothers of your children who feel abandoned, your mothers feel you have taken them for granted and that you have taken advantage of their love for you. Before you can become the king that God wants you to be, you have to mend those relationships. The best way to do that is forgiveness. You have to ask for it and those you are asking have to be willing to give it. You can begin by asking God to forgive you of your shortcomings, then forgive yourself for the mistakes you have made in your life.

Forgiveness is the cure for a diseased relationship. But, just like Penicillin takes time to cure completely, sometimes so does forgiveness. You may have to ask for forgiveness many times before the person you are asking actually responds. If the person you need forgiveness from, fails to accept your apology, understand that it is that person's right and decision. But also know that once you have made every effort to mend the relationship, then you will no longer be held responsible if the recipient of your request for forgiveness does not receive your apology.

There was an occasion in my life where I was put in a position where I had to forgive. I was in my kitchen, mixing a cake and preparing it for baking when I received a phone call from my friend. My friend, before I could say anything, cursed me out and hung up in my face! I was flabbergasted! The things that I was accused of were untrue! I felt that the verbal assault that I received, from someone who supposedly cared about me, was unjustified.

With my heart in my hand and my emotions on my shoulders, I went back to stirring my cake mix as tears filled my eyes! I was so upset by the accusations. I said to myself that I would never do anything intentionally to hurt my friend and I couldn't understand why she would be so rude to me. While I was there having my pity party, a voice spoke to me and said, "Call her back and apologize." I immediately resisted, saying, "God, you must be crazy! I didn't do anything! I'm not the one who cursed somebody out! She owes me the apology!"

The voice said again, "Call her back and apologize."

At that point, I went to praying and I received more from the Spirit of the Lord than I had hoped for. Instead of relieving me of my responsibility, I was further advised that there must have been something that I'd done that would cause my friend to use such harsh words against me. I also understood that by apologizing and asking for forgiveness, I was setting myself free from the bondage that my friend was setting me up for.

So, in obedience to God, I called my friend back and offered a heartfelt apology for something I didn't do. She quickly accepted my apology and hung up in my face again! This time, instead of crying, I just rejoiced. I understood that I was no longer in bondage, but my friend was! No, I was not rejoicing because my friend had to bear the burden of our relationship, I was rejoicing because after I apologized and asked for forgiveness, the *burden* of the relationship was not on me! After that incident, I was able to be in my friend's presence and not feel embarrassed or uncomfortable.

    <u>Where you are today has nothing to do with where you could be tomorrow. However, *what* you do while you are where you are can determine how *long* you will be where you are.</u> Remember the lawn cutting boy who bought the car dealership? I wrote my first book in 2002. When things didn't go as well as I dreamed, I could have stopped there. I remember telling my husband that I wanted to be a *successful* writer. My husband cleverly responded, "When you finished writing the book, you became a successful writer, baby." His statement changed my whole outlook! Whereas I was to the point where I didn't want to write anymore, my perspective changed and writing continued to be the passion that fueled my life! My goal is to write as many books as God will allow me and bless me to write! Only a few short years later, I have personally published five books. This one is my sixth! The only way I can reach my goal is by pursuing it! In 2002, I was just starting. Had I not pursued the goal, today, I would only have the one book published and you would not be reading this one. But, my persistence in writing and pursuing my dream has gotten me to the place where I am today. If you want something badly enough, you can get there. How long it takes you to reach your goal will be determined by the amount of work you are willing to dedicate to the pursuit of your dream.

Integrity; doing the right thing simply because it is the right thing to do. If you want to be a man of integrity, all you have to do is begin with the small things. Remember the last time someone gave you extra change at the store? Did you give it back or did you excuse yourself by saying it was your *blessing*? When you get to the place in your life where the little things become important to you, then the big things will be easy.

Being a man of integrity means being in a position where someone talks about you and they can't come up with anything evil. If you always operate on a level of integrity, you won't have to worry about negative feedback. Integrity will take you a lot further than dishonesty. Integrity will take you higher than pride. Integrity will bring you a return greater than any monetary investment you would ever make. To measure the integrity of your actions, just ask yourself the question, "What would Jesus do in this situation?" And respond the same way that He would.

Integrity is doing the right thing when others are looking and when others are not looking. Integrity means saying "Please" and "Thank you", just because it's right and good. Integrity means saying "excuse me", and integrity doesn't push or shove or honk its horn angrily in heavy traffic. A man of integrity won't go to the express line with a buggy full of items. No, it's not a crime, per se, it's just right and good. If you always do the right thing, you won't have to worry about the things that you do.

Change your mind, you can change your life. Begin by changing the way you think about yourself. There are many of you who have low self esteem because of things you have done in the past and because of things that have happened to you. There are things you have had control over and there are some things that you didn't have control of. Regardless of what your past is, you still have the opportunity to be and do all that you have ever dreamed of being and doing.

I challenge you to draw a line down the middle of the page. Label one side: *Things I like about myself.* Label the other side: *Things I don't like about myself.* Then, list things about you on both sides of the paper that fit into the appropriate category.

Don't forget to list the things that are on the inside of you, as well as some of those things that are physical. Some of the things you like about yourself could include your creative imagination, you have a good sense of humor, you like doing things for people, you make people laugh. You can also include things like punctuality, self assured, confident, you like to sew, you are a good athlete, you may like to write poetry, or you may be able to sing, you might enjoy dancing. You can also include things like your smile, you like the way your hair looks, people compliment you on the way you dress, etc.

After you have finished listing the things you like about yourself, list things on the opposite side of the paper, making reference to those things that you dislike about yourself. You may dislike your present weight condition. You may not like the fact that you can't sing or dance. You may have a sickness that limits your abilities. You may be one who stutters or you are unable to speak in front of a crowd. You may be disgusted with yourself because of your inability to save money and be a good steward of what God has given to you. It does not matter what you list under this column. All that matters is that you be true to yourself by listing those things about yourself that you are dissatisfied with. When you finish, take a look at both sides. Are they a true picture of you? If you need to make changes or additions, do so.

The next step is to review the things you like about you. This represents your self-esteem! You probably esteem yourself more than you think! These are the things that you should focus on. It may be true that you may not be able to do some things, you may not have some things, but, nevertheless, there is always something good about you! Be happy with who you are!

Look at your list of things you do not like about yourself. Make new columns on another sheet of paper. Transfer those things you don't like about yourself to the new sheet. Now, make notations next to each item. Identify those things that you can change or that are changeable. Make a notation next to the things you cannot change such as your age. For those things you cannot change, write the word, "ACCEPT". The things about you that you cannot change are things that you will have to accept. You can't change the fact that you have big feet, so just accept the truth about you. Know that it's okay for your feet to be big!

Look at the other things on your list. Identify those things that you can change. List in the column next to that item what it would take to change the situation. You may want and need to lose weight. That is something you can change. List the things you would need to do in order to make that change. Some of those things might include getting a physical examination so that you will lose weight intelligently. You will need to cut back on the foods you eat. You will need to exercise more. You will need to be tenacious, focused, disciplined, consistent, persistent and you will need to persevere. Lastly, ask yourself the question, "Am I willing to do what I need to do in order to bring about this change in my life?" If your answer is "yes", then you have already started a plan of action. Your next step would be to put your plan into action. You could begin by praying and asking God to help you be healthier in your eating habits.

If you answer "no", then your only recourse is to accept the things in your life that you would otherwise think you need to change, because your situation is not going to change if you are not willing to put forth the effort to make it change.

One more thing I want to mention in regards to changing your mind and changing your life. Take your current situation, for example. If you are in a job situation that is uncomfortable and you cannot afford to leave your job, then in order to make your situation more bearable, you may have to make some personal adjustments. If, after you have tried everything and you still can't change your situation, change your perspective.

Chapter 19

THERE *IS* HOPE!

*O*n June 17, 2007, during our regular church service, six gang members offered their hands to our pastor. They gave their lives to Christ!

Since meeting these young men, I've had to change my perspective on some things.

While our congregation was trying to psychoanalyze them, reprogram them and change their way of thinking, they were teaching and reprogramming us merely by their presence.

There was an occasion when one of the younger boys overheard one of the prominent men in our congregation use profanity while inside the church. When the boys returned home, the young fellow used profanity at the house. When Easton chastised him, he offered his rebuttal, "Why you sweating me? That man at the church was cussing and he was at the church!"

I told one of my friends that, "these young men are going to teach us church folks how to be Christians."

I asked a group of offenders why they thought young boys

would join a gang in the first place. Their responses were ones that I expected. These are some of the things they said: for love, camaraderie, companionship, stability, someone they can lean on and trust, strength, guidance, direction, encouragement, a father figure, these are just a few. Then, I asked them why were they seeking these things and the response again was what I expected, "Because they aren't getting it at home." Finally, I asked, "Who should be giving them these things?" They responded, almost unanimously, "We should, their fathers."

The reality of this book hit me like an arrow through a bull's-eye when I left my position with the Texas adult prison system and started working on a Texas juvenile correctional facility. My first day on the job, it took all the strength that I could muster to keep my mouth from falling open and my eyes free from tears. All around me there were young African-American men—lost boys. As I began my work and as I heard the stories, I realized that many of these young men were the victims of a fatherless and sometimes motherless childhood. They have been abandoned, abused, beaten, raped, and stripped of hope. Their stories are an endless horror. But, the bottom line, for all of them, regardless of their race or their age is they just want to be loved.

One of the young boys brought me to tears when he shouted to his case worker, "I don't want you to care about me! I want my momma to love me and care about me the way you do! I want my daddy to care about me! Where's he at? Why don't he love me?"

It was at that point that I realized that the youth, all distraught, angry, and violent, was not acting out because he was just a terrible person, but he was hurting in a way that he could not explain. He just wanted to be loved—by him mother and his father! Too many times, we look at the outward behavior and never question what's going on in the heart!

There is hope because all of our young African-American brothers are not all *bad!* Sometimes, they've just had bad things happen to them. There is hope because the young men who joined our church are still coming, they are bringing others to join our church family, and the ones who are coming are also laying their flags down. There is hope because these young men have even crossed lines of gang affiliation to bring others to Christ!

There is hope because there are many, many African-American men who are being released from prisons across our nation and they are not returning! Instead, they are educating themselves, maturing, learning new skills, and they are refusing to be a part of the statistical system that has labeled them as failures! There are many of our African-American men who are taking their places in our lives. To them, I say, "Thank you! We love you!"

Chapter 20

ONE MORE THING

❧   ❧

*T*o the successful women, I congratulate you on your climb to the top! You deserve a serious pat on the back. As a professional, educated, strong, self-determined, disciplined, African-American woman myself, I know that your struggle has not been easy. It has not been easy getting the promotion you deserve. It hasn't been easy rearing your children. It has not been easy for you to achieve all of your dreams and goals. I know that there have been many days that you have gone without. One thing that I have learned is that no matter how successful we become, no matter how much money we obtain or how much education we get, at the end of the day, we just want to be loved for who we are.

To all of the successful African-American brothers out there, you are our heroes! If you have graduated from college, let me applaud you! If you stayed in college without using or selling drugs, you are to be admired. If you have obtained your success by starting your own business, let me know! I will help you get the word out! If you are a father to your children, if you were more than just a sperm donor to the woman (or women) who have given birth to your offspring, then you deserve a standing ovation! For all of the faithful African-American husbands, thank you for helping us build strong families. Without you, our children would be the ones who *lose.*

For all of the brothers who don't mind taking the "dirty" jobs just to get the job at home done, you deserve a raise! For every brother who wants more out of life than just another "hookup" or fast money, I pray that the Lord will bless all of your hard work. For all of the brothers who have made their mark in life by living up to your full potential, we are standing on your shoulders. Remember this one thing; it does not matter what you do or how you do it, all that matters is that you have acted with integrity so that you and your children will be proud of the work that you have done. Also remember, in all that you do, our children are looking at you! Our children want to be just like you!

To all of the "substitute" fathers, godfathers, step-fathers, play fathers and father figures, I thank you! I thank you and commend you for stepping up and stepping in. Because of you, there are many children who will not fall into the traps that destroy us. There are many African-American children who will be reared in an environment that is conducive to their success. The many men who take time out to talk to our young people constantly remind them and us that all African-American brothers are not *bad.*

Unfortunately, there are too many African-American men who do not meet the mark, so to speak. It is these men that I am speaking to in the greater portion of this book. It is time for all of us to take a long hard look at where we are, where we have been, and where we need to be. After our real self-examination, we should begin taking steps to better ourselves as a race of people in these United States. The first step towards our success and our future should begin in our own homes, with our families, with our children, with our spouses, with our parents, and in our relationships with the same.

Some who read this book may think that I am begging for the attention of African-American men. Begging puts me in the mind of making my request strictly for my own benefit. Pleading with you for you to change is done on your behalf and for your benefit. My purpose in this message is to encourage you, compel you, and constrain you to pull yourself up! If I see someone drowning and I offer them a rope and plead with them to grab hold of it, I am not doing it to save myself, but I am doing it to save the one who is drowning. Unfortunately, for us as African-American women, when African-American men drown so do we.

If you love us, then show us! Remember in Chapter 12 where I stated that love is a word that requires action? If you love us, let your actions speak louder than your words. If you love us, stop killing yourselves and stop killing each other. If you love us, stop seducing our sons into your world of drugs, gangs, violence, homosexuality, and sexually immoral behavior. If you love us, quit causing our children to be orphans because of your absence. Stop making children if you don't want to be responsible for them! Don't sleep with an African-American woman if you don't love her enough to get married. It's just right and good.

If you love us, stop lying to us, stop cheating on us, and stop taking from us without giving in return! Stop being unfaithful to us! Stop abandoning us! Stop infecting us with your deadly diseases and habits! Don't take your mother's hard earned money and savings account and squander it away without her knowledge. If you love us, don't steal, don't kill, and don't destroy. If you love us, don't take our love for you for granted. Say what you mean and mean what you say. Don't hate or hurt your fellow African-American brother!

We love you and just want to be loved by you. Mothers and wives are crying. Daughters are depressed and sons are becoming victims of your madness. My African-American brothers, you are on a vicious merry go round and the only way this life threatening cycle will stop is if you get off of it and become the men that you were created to be. Whatever you choose to do or be, remember, your son wants to be just like you and your daughter wants to marry a man just like you!

I am not naïve. I know that there will be some who agree with the things I have written in this book and there will be many who will disagree. There will also be some who will become angry with the things I have revealed. But, as I think I have already stated, I have been working in the Criminal Justice arena, in the area of incarcerated felons, juvenile and adult alike, for over twenty years! Not much has changed even though I have witnessed three generations of African-American males make their way through the Texas penal system! It is a tragedy that desperately needs to be addressed! Who better to address it than one who has experienced the pain? Who better to address it than one who knows, understands and at the same time, has compassion for our African-American brothers?

There was a man that I met when I first began working for the Texas Department of Corrections, in 1987, while I was assigned to the Ellis

I Unit. Twenty years later, in 2007, I saw him again, at the facility I was employed at during that time. This facility is located in Beaumont, Texas. When I saw him in 1987, he was already in the process of serving a 27 year sentence. Since his offense was aggravated, he was going to serve out most of that sentence before being released on parole. When I saw him in 2007, he confessed that his son was an infant when he was first incarcerated and by 2007, his son was a grown man, married and with children of his own. The man also confessed that he greatly regretted not being there to help the mother of his son. It is to this man, his son, his ex-wife, and the many like them, that I am offering these few words of encouragement. If your life is perfect, then throw your hands in the air, lay your head back, and give God some praise!

I am aware that I will be criticized and ridiculed by many, but I may also be complimented and applauded by at least a few because of the words I have offered on these pages. Nevertheless, I cannot be concerned about the results, because I am responsible to God. He has given me the gift to write and He has called me to minister. All that I can do, after all has been said and done, is offer this prayer, "Let the words of my mouth and the meditation of my heart be acceptable in Your sight, O Lord, my strength and my redeemer," (Psalm 19:14).

I close this book, with this benediction: May the blessing of the Lord overtake you, even as you pursue Him. May His grace ever abound in your life. May His mercy be never-ending and His love be ever-flowing. May He bless you with His favor. Keep the lamp of your life held high, for there are many who follow your light! "Now to Him who is able to do exceedingly abundantly above all that we ask or think, according to the power that works in us, to Him be glory in the church by Christ Jesus to all generations, forever and ever. Amen." (Ephesians 3:20, 21).

www.ingramcontent.com/pod-product-compliance
Lightning Source LLC
LaVergne TN
LVHW011326080426
835513LV00006B/214